porsche turbo
The Full History of the Race and Production Cars

Photographer
Peter Vann
Authors
Clauspeter Becker, Malte Jürgens, Michael Köckritz, Eckhard Schimpf

Topping the Bill

Be prepared to meet a leading member of today's 'performance society' on the following pages: the Porsche Turbo. For Porsche, the Turbo as the top model in its program is of very special significance, because it is one of the principal exhibits that back up our claim to technical authority in automobile design and development. A quarter of a century ago, Porsche introduced the turbocharger to the sports car and has since then, with its successive Turbo models, maintained a leading position in the small, elite group of truly fast, high-performance sports cars.

But the Turbo also has an authentic economic background. It is not an exotic design manufactured only in small numbers, but a genuine production model produced in moderately large volume and intended to make a profit for our company. I freely admit that we and our shareholders earn more from the sale of a Turbo than from any other model. The Turbo rewards its purchaser, however, with an unsurpassed ability to arouse the emotions. Anyone who has ever driven a Turbo is full of enthusiasm for this remarkable car, and most other members of the public also acknowledge its perfection or declare it to be their 'dream car'. Unlike its rivals, the Turbo communicates its prestige in a very personal manner. The driver too is included in the impression of functional efficiency and technical competence that it creates. This enhances the car's appeal and explains why the driver is seldom exposed to aggressive, envious feelings on the part of those not fortunate enough to drive such a car.

Another Turbo characteristic that is rated highly by our customers when they in turn wish to sell the car is its high secondhand value. It is surely one of the very few cars around that can offer a quarter of a century of loyal service to its owners and be just as much fun to drive as on the day it first took to the road. It therefore comes as no surprise to find Porsche Turbos from the first model generation still commanding a good price.

The Porsche Turbo has entered a further phase of its career in 2000, with the appearance of a new model, and I am convinced that it can look forward to a future even longer than the 25 years of success it has already enjoyed.

Dr. Wendelin Wiedeking

Turbo rules —
25 years of thrusting ahead

1   **It All Began with Büchi**
How a Swiss inventor developed the turbocharger in 1905 and needed 20 years to make it run   **9**

The Pressure of the Early Years   **2**
15   How Hans Mezger became the father of all Porsche Turbos

3   **Open-ended Thrust**
What it's like to drive a thousand horsepower. The Porsche 917/30's success story   **23**

The Power that came out of the Crisis   **4**
37   The first Turbo appeared at an inappropriate moment

5   **A Very Mild Expression of Power**
500 horsepower meet 800 kilograms: the 934 in 1976 and 1977   **47**

When the Pressure is On   **6**
53   The 959: the multi-stage turbo engine, a dramatic three-acter

7   **Hero of a Long-running Series**
25 years as the perfect 'business express'   **64**

Air Power for Le Mans   **8**
77   Success for the six-cylinder turbo engine in the world's most famous 24-hour motor race

9   **The Way to the Very Top**
Statements from the Weissach 'think tank'   **87**

Snatched from the Air   **10**
97   Aerodynamics for safe driving at 300 kilometers an hour

11   **3,000 Kilometers a Day**
Top speed as an everyday event. A report from Nardo   **103**

Let the Processor Play Professor   **12**
115   Porsche Stability Management makes fast driving safer

13   **External Influences**
Advertising and communication: How Porsche speaks   **123**

A Day with a Thousand Curves   **14**
131   To drive or be driven - preferably by Walter Röhrl

15   **Stout Hearts and New Horizons**
Flexing the muscles for a journey into the future   **143**

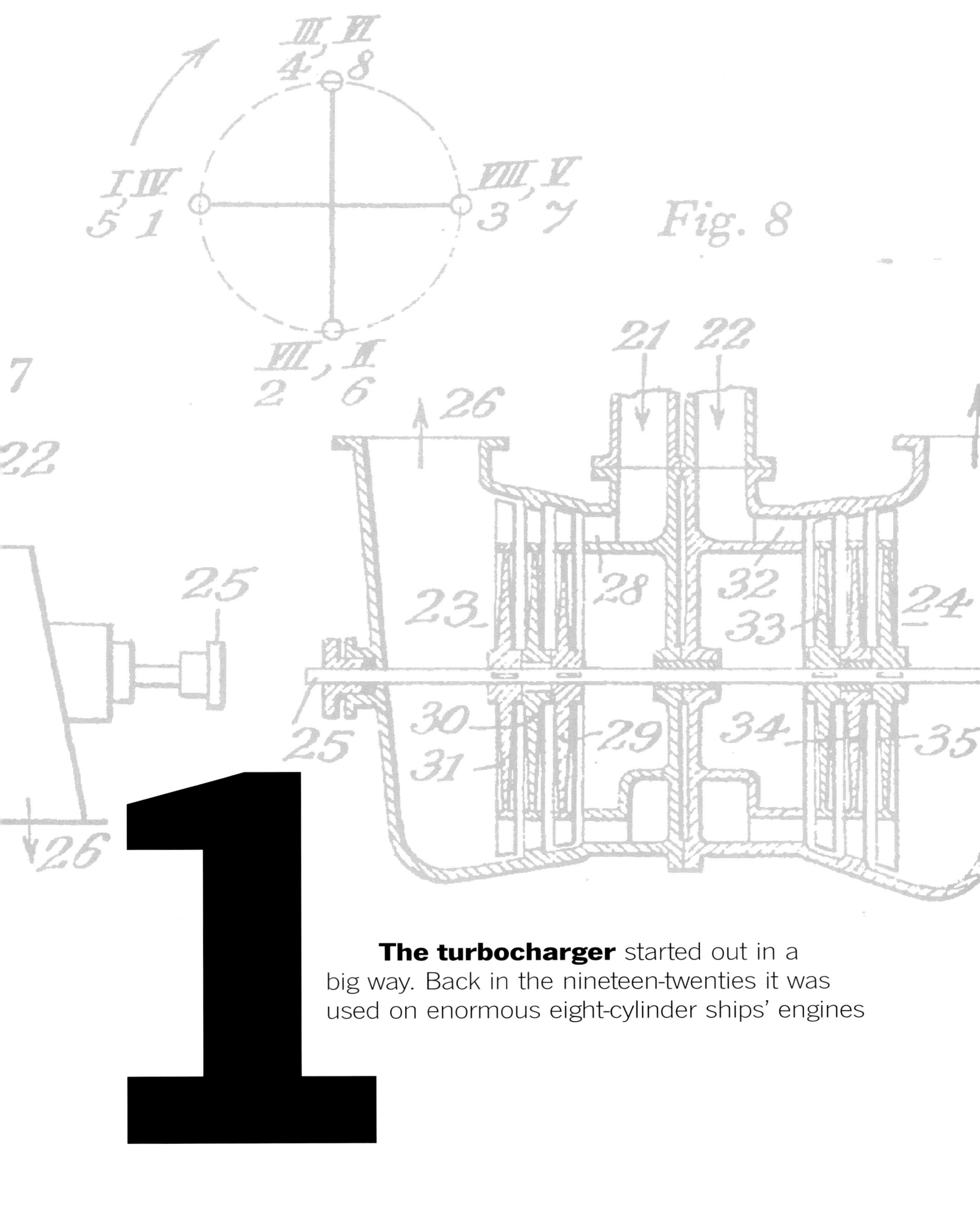

1

The turbocharger started out in a big way. Back in the nineteen-twenties it was used on enormous eight-cylinder ships' engines

SCHWEIZERISCHE EIDGENOSSENSCHAFT

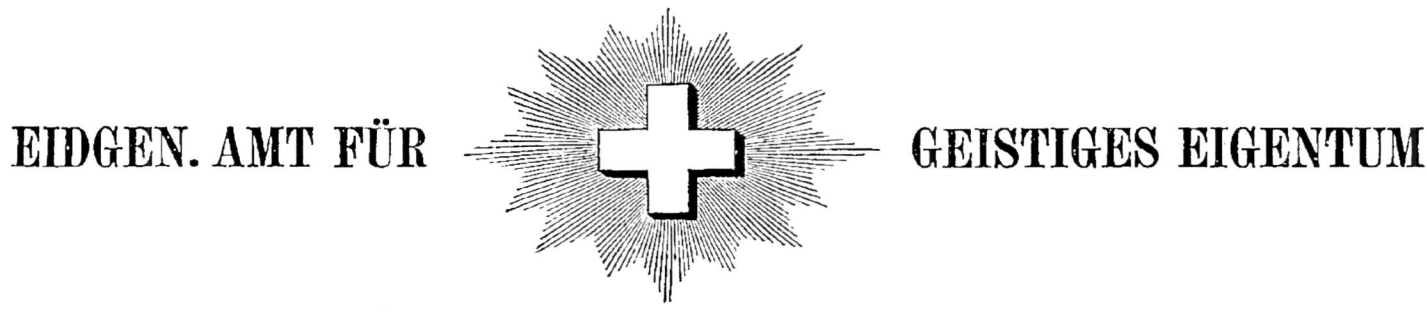

EIDGEN. AMT FÜR GEISTIGES EIGENTUM

PATENTSCHRIFT

Veröffentlicht am 1. Oktober 1927

Nr. 122664 (Gesuch eingereicht: 30. November 1925, 12 Uhr.) Klasse **104**a

HAUPTPATENT

Alfred BÜCHI, Winterthur (Schweiz).

Verbrennungskraftmaschine.

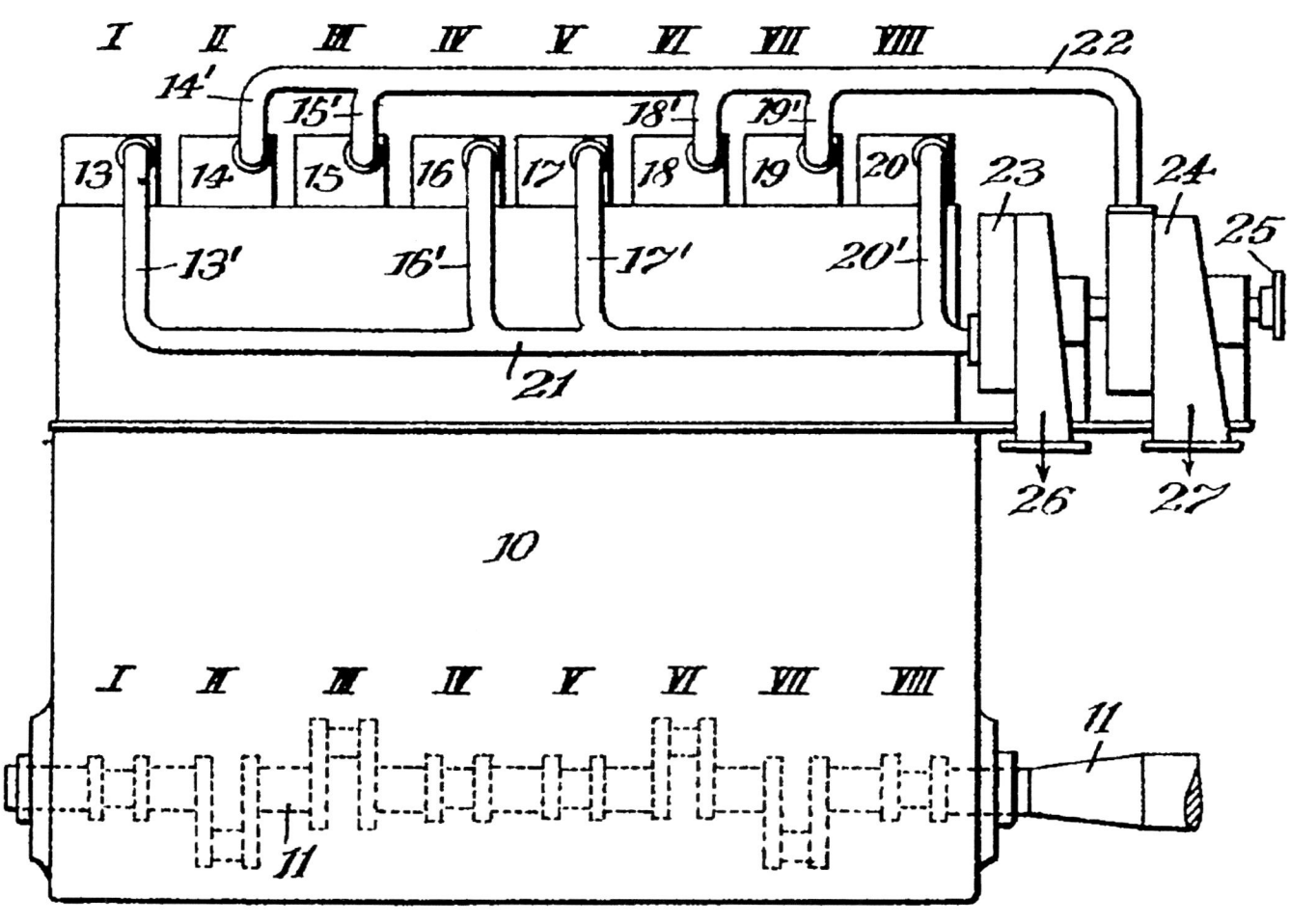

Chapter 1

THE TURBOCHARGER WAS ALREADY 70 YEARS OLD when the first Porsche Turbo cars left their own short assembly line in the Zuffenhausen district of Stuttgart, Germany. The first patents for this type of forced aspiration system were issued in November 1905: one on the thirteenth in the USA, another three days later by the Imperial Patent Office of the German Reich.

It was a Swiss engineer, Dr. Alfred Büchi, who first had the idea of using the energy in the exhaust gas from an internal combustion engine, which otherwise escapes uselessly to the atmosphere. He was a graduate of the much-respected Cantonal College of Advanced Technology in Zürich, where many years later two further advocates of the turbocharging principle would also study: Michael May and Ferdinand Piëch.

Alfred Büchi's patent application depicted a design that we would be amazed at today: a radial four-cycle spark-ignition unit with eight cylinders and a central eccentric shaft connected rigidly to the exhaust-driven turbine at the left and the charge-air impeller at the right. The turbocharging elements are very large, not only because of the limited running speed of this kind of reciprocating engine but also because Büchi planned to run it at very high boost pressures of three to four bar, with a pressure of 16 bar built up ahead of the exhaust-side turbine.

The inventor's original concept envisaged using the remaining third of the energy that would normally escape from the exhaust pipe not only to improve cylinder filling as we do today, but also for direct propulsion purposes. The modern mechanical engineer would certainly comment that Büchi had discovered a legitimate principle, but had hoped to achieve more than was possible in practice – not an efficient overall solution.

IT ALL BEGAN WITH BÜCHI

How a Swiss inventor developed the turbocharger in 1905 - and needed 20 years to make it run

By Clauspeter Becker

As an employee of the Gebrüder Sulzer engine manufacturing company in Winterthur, Switzerland, Dr. Büchi found the ideal application for his invention in due course. His experiments between 1911 and 1914 were dedicated to the company's own specialty – diesel engines. The results laid down two fundamental rules for modern turbocharging: the turbine and impeller are only used to boost the charge of mixture or air entering the cylinders, and they are not mechanically driven by the engine. In the final concept, the boost pressure on the inlet side is higher than the back pressure ahead of the exhaust-driven turbine. When this principle was granted a German patent in November 1915, Europe was already deeply embroiled in the First World War.

The turbocharger received its next stimulus in 1923. The German Transport Ministry commissioned the passenger vessels 'Preussen' and 'City of Hamburg' from the Vulkan shipyard in Hamburg, for service to the East Prussian ports. Each was to be driven by two ten-cylinder four-cycle diesel engines. These were built by Vulkan under license from M.A.N., and had their power output increased from 1,750 to 2,500 horsepower by the addition of an exhaust-driven turbocharger. Dr. Büchi designed these devices, and was thus able to reap the reward of twenty years of brilliant thinking and development work.

Back in the 1920s, Büchi was hard at work establishing the rules for modern turbocharging technology. In 1925 he patented the pressure-wave process, with a divided exhaust system and double-flow turbine. In the course of his work for the Swiss Locomotive and Machinery Company (SLM) in Winterthur, he even planned a large four-cylinder turbocharged engine with a charge-air intercooler.

Chapter 1

It was another ten years before the German State Railroad began to operate its first turbocharged diesel locomotive, with the impressive power output of 1,400 horsepower. At this time the turbocharger remained a Swiss specialty, as evidenced by the Sulzer company in 1938, when it began series production of a truck with turbocharged diesel engine.

Even after the Second World War, the turbocharger found it difficult to make the jump to the automobile or sports car. In 1962 it was General Motors in the USA that displayed the necessary courage and willingness to take a risk, by introducing not one but two new turbocharged models.

The Chevrolet Corvair Monza, with an air-cooled flat-six engine at the back, developed 180 horsepower from 2.7 liters at the peak of its development in 1966; all in all, no fewer than 60,000 of these cars were sold.

The Oldsmobile F 85 Jetfire with its turbocharged 5.4-liter V8 engine had an output of 260 hp. Both cars suffered from a number of problems that led to severe doubts as to the suitability of the new power-raising principle. After only two years, the management of General Motors decided to stop using the turbocharger on its Oldsmobiles, though the rear-engined Chevrolet, with its flat-six engine recalling the Porsche design, continued with this form of power unit until 1966.

It was also in the 1960s that another Swiss engineer began to take an interest in the turbocharger. Michael May, who was employed by Porsche between 1961 and 1962, started work as an independent tuner in 1967

10

Büchi's 75-year-old patents contain everything that has appeared in turbocharger technology until the present day, including the 'twin turbo' principle and the resonant air intake system

In his first Imperial German patent application of 1905, Büchi describes a compound eight-cylinder radial engine and exhaust-driven turbine, with the latter not only boosting combustion air intake but also contributing to the tractive power – too much of a good thing, as was to be proved

and tackled the strongly built Ford V6 engines, with their cast iron blocks, as his first project. A simple turbocarger kit costing 3,000 German Marks transformed the 2.3-liter unit's power output from 108 to 180 horsepower. Admittedly, the power and torque curves were unsuitably 'peaky' in a way we now condemn as 'typically turbo'. But May's tuned Ford Capri models went surprisingly well, and helped to associate the turbocharger in the potential customer's mind with such terms as power and dynamism.

The nineteen-seventies were evidently ripe for the breakthrough into the era of the turbocharger. Much of the impetus came from the third of our graduates from the College of Advanced Technology in Zürich, Ferdinand Piëch. As manager of Porsche's competition department in 1968 he decided to build a twelve-cylinder racing engine as a means of achieving the so far elusive victory in the Le Mans 24-hour race. In 1971, by the time his cars had crossed the finishing line victorious for the second time, turbocharging had made their engines into the most powerful units in the history of motor sport. The triumphant roar of the Porsche 917/30's engine in the American CanAm series was a message understood all over the world: the turbocharger was at last on its way to the top.

12

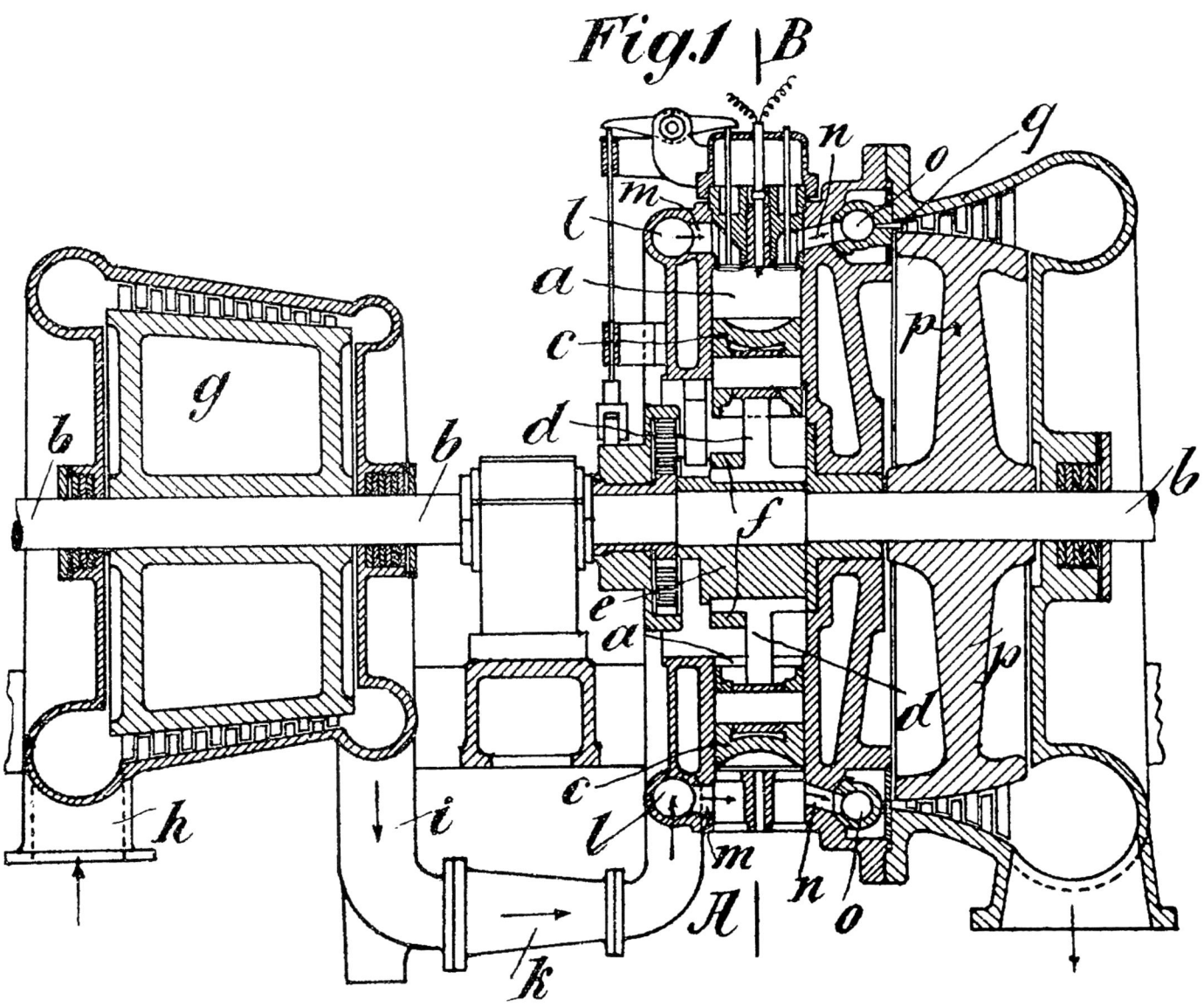

Alfred J. Büchi

was born on July 11, 1879, and it is quite possible that his career was decided in the cradle, since his father was factory manager at the Sulzer mechanical engineering plant in Winterthur. From 1899 to 1904 he studied in Zürich at the Cantonal College of Advanced Technology, then worked for industrial companies in Belgium and England as well as experimenting with his exhaust-driven turbocharging concept, for which he was awarded various patents.

Büchi returned to Switzerland in 1908, was taken on by Sulzer in Wetzikon and soon rose to be head of the diesel-engine research department. After the First World War, he was employed at the Howaldtswerke shipyards in Kiel, Germany, but soon returned to his native country and worked for the Swiss Locomotive and Machinery company (SLM) in Winterthur, where he became a director in 1926. In the same year he founded the Büchi Syndicate, with SLM and also Brown Boveri & Cie of Baden as members.

In 1935 Alfred Büchi retired and devoted himself as a freelance engineer to further study of the turbocharger, his life's work. The Zürich College granted him an honorary doctorate in 1938. Büchi continued to run his consulting engineers' office until his death on October 27, 1959.

2

The TAG turbocharged engine
of 1983 is Hans Mezger's masterpiece

THE PRESSURE OF THE EA

By Clauspeter Becker

HANS MEZGER

The father of all Porsche Turbos: "It all started with the 1,000-horsepower CanAm engine"

Chapter 2

RLY YEARS

HANS MEZGER'S EARLY YEARS were fortunately not disturbed too much by the events of the Second World War. Born in Ottmersheim, not far from Ludwigsburg in South Germany in November 1929, he was a conscientious schoolchild, passing his higher school leaving and university entrance exam in 1949 at the Friedrich Schiller Gymnasium in Ludwigsburg, and gaining his diploma as a graduate in mechanical engineering from the College of Advanced Technology in Stuttgart in 1956.

No employment problems faced the new Dipl.-Ing. Mezger – he had several job offers from industry. Instead of taking one of these up, he applied to a company that was not seeking new recruits from the universities: Porsche, and was offered a job in the tractor department.

Experience gained with the CanAm twelve-cylinder engine was of immediate benefit to the flat six unit for the 911 (the drawings in the picture are for this engine)

This would have involved working on diesel engines for the tractors that Porsche still made in those days. Mezger was courageous enough to refuse this offer, and was rewarded with a job in the calculation department, which thereby increased in size from two to three people.

At that time, complex mathematical problems were solved with the aid of table-top calculating machines, later with punched-card equipment from IBM. The calculations were by no means easy: development of the four-cylinder engine from the early Carrera, for example, with its valve gear driven by four vertical shafts and four overhead camshafts. The individual cam profiles and those of the cam followers that actuated the valves all had to converted into mathematical formulae.

Straight from technical college, the young Mezger discovered to his amazement: "At that time, we had to tackle problems like these empirically. Our camshaft supplier, the Schleicher company in Munich, used to arrive at the most suitable cam and follower profiles by making scale models five times larger than the real thing!"

Hans Mezger resolved to perform this task by mathematical methods. Up to 60,000 calculations – which a modern computer could dispatch in a matter of seconds – were needed before the final formula was arrived at. Driven by ambition, the young engineer then solved a problem concerning valve springs that was crucial to the success of Porsche's competition cars, after which it was obvious where he belonged: in the Racing

Chapter 2

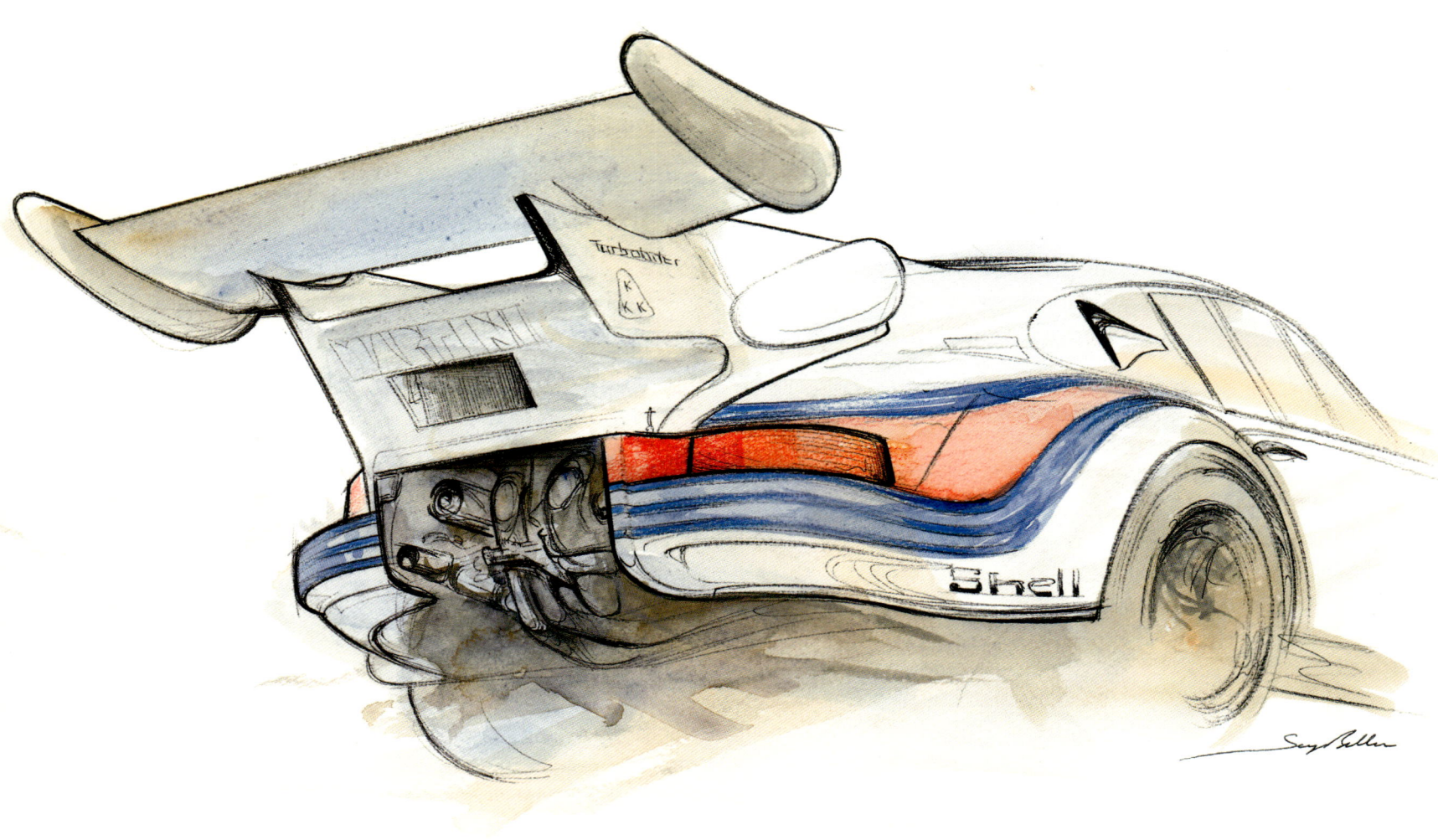

Porsche Carrera Turbo RSR, 1974

Department. From 1960 to 1962 he took a hand in the brief career of Porsche's flat-eight Formula 1 engine, with which Dan Gurney did indeed win one Grand Prix race, in Rouen, France. Mezger sums up this engine, the scourge of all racing mechanics, concisely: "It was simply too complicated!"

"The Racing Department was the fire service that had to leap into action when there were problems on the production cars", says Mezger, commenting on the next phase of his Porsche career. When the 911 was first exhibited at the Germany Motor Show in Frankfurt in 1963, its engine was still far from the series-production maturity and perfection that people were expecting. Together with Dr. Porsche's young nephew Ferdinand Piëch, Mezger took the 901 engine, as it was designated internally, under his wing. It was given a crankshaft with eight instead of five main bearings and also converted to dry sump lubrication.

The next project was a development of the 911 engine with four overhead camshafts. Although this never went into series production, it

In 1974 the Porsche 911 RSR gave the turbocharged engine a successful start on European racetracks. When overtaking its rivals it gave them a glimpse of where its superior performance came from: the turbocharger under the big rear wing

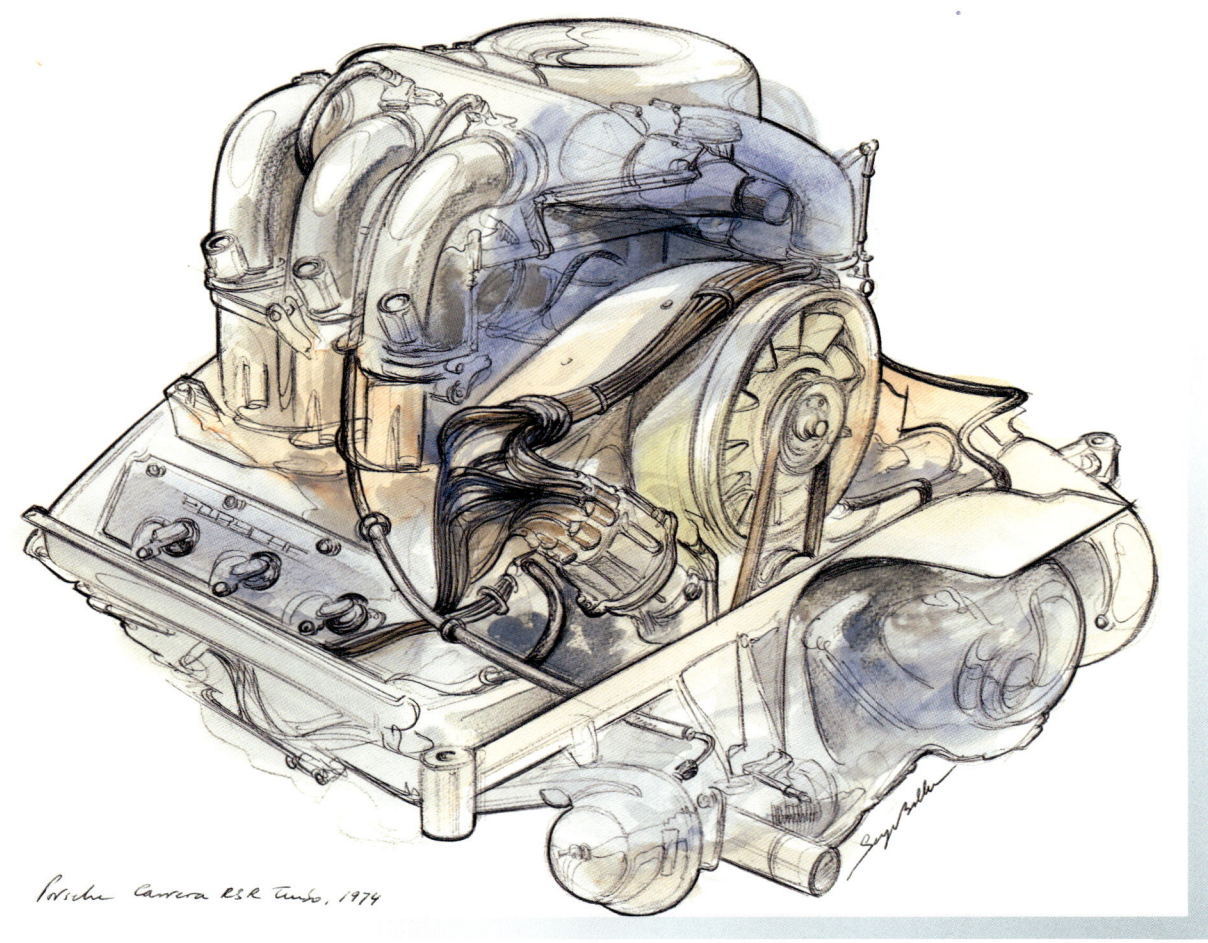

Porsche Carrera RSR Turbo, 1974

THE 2.1 RSR TURBO

The RSR's six-cylinder 'boxer' engine had a surprising resemblance to the standard production unit. From a swept volume of 2.1 liters, it developed 500 horsepower at an engine speed of 8,000 rpm – thanks to turbocharging

was a useful source of components for the competition engines for many years to come. The first derivative, an eight-cylinder unit, was highly successful. It was not until the 917's twelve-cylinder version appeared that major changes to the crankshaft and engine block were needed – but this monumental engine deservedly has the following chapter of this book to itself.

Hans Mezger's successful engines furthered his career, and after running the company's competition engine development program he soon assumed responsibility for every technical aspect of the cars.

After a most impressive debut in the CanAm series, racing engine design work reverted to near-series versions of the six-cylinder units. Mezger became aware of the limits of air cooling at a very early stage: experimental four-valve cylinder heads proved unsatisfactory and had to be discarded. Initial experiments with water cooling were highly promising: by 1977 the 3.2-liter turbocharged engines were delivering between 700

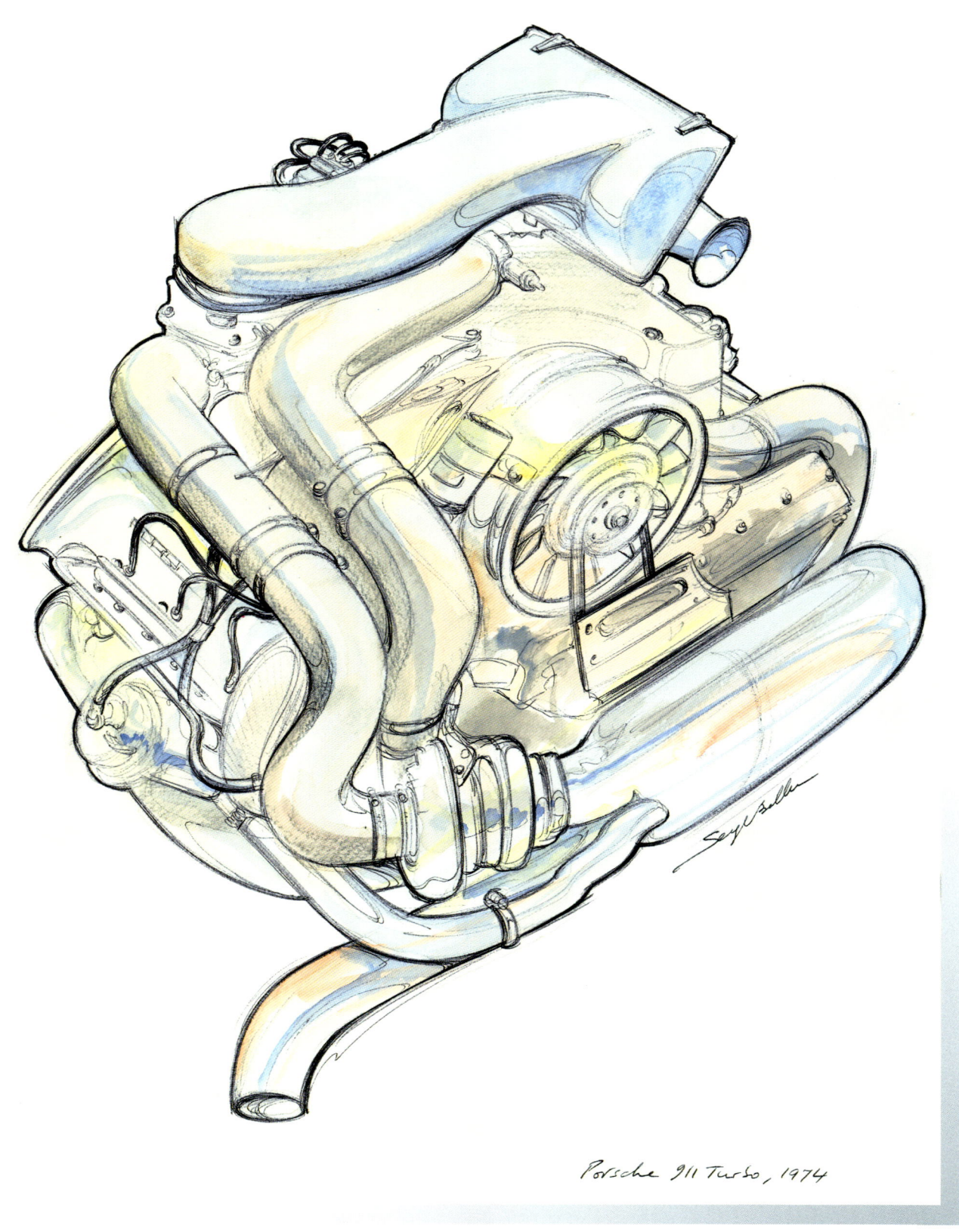

Porsche 911 Turbo, 1974

THE TURBO – 1974 VINTAGE

Chapter 2

Porsche 911 Turbo, 1974

The bulging cheeks over the wheels of the RSR and its rear spoiler were unmistakable visual features of the Porsche Turbo from 1974 on. The air-cooled flat-six engine began its turbocharged career with a displacement of three liters and an output of 260 hp

and 800 horsepower, and even then test rig observers were convinced that there was more to come. The basic 911 engine, combined with the turbocharging principle, revealed its unexpected potential best of all in the smallest version that was ever built. For the German Motor Sport Championship, in which most of the contenders had naturally aspirated two-liter engines, Porsche produced a smaller version of its turbocharged engine. Because of the handicap factor of 1.4 applied to forced-aspitation units, it had a displacement of only 1,428 cc. None the less, this 'baby boxer' was delivering not far short of 500 horsepower, a figure of which the first three-liter Formula 1 engines would have been proud in the late 1970s

"Even then, we were thinking about building a Formula 1 engine," Mezger recalls. Technical Director Ernst Fuhrmann, however, was not convinced of the chances of the reduced-size, turbocharged unit.

Chapter 2

His view was that the 1.4 handicap factor gave it a certain chance, but that more severe 2.0 factor in Formula 1 would give the Porsche engine no real chance of success against the normally-aspitated competition. Renault did in fact run a turbocharged engine in Formula 1 from 1977 on, but its performance was initially most disappointing and two years elapsed before its first victory. Despite this unpromising background, Hans Mezger encouraged a Stuttgart Technical University graduate to write a thesis on the '1.5-liter forced-aspiration V6 engine for Formula 1'.

Before long, inquiries for an engine of this kind were being received from outside sources. The racing driver Willibald Kauhsen asked Porsche to quote him a price, and in August 1981 Ron Dennis und John Barnard from McLaren contacted Porsche with the same aim in mind. Mezger and Barnard, however, soon decided that a developed version of the 'baby boxer' would not be suitable and that only a V6 would satisfy the demands of Formula 1 racing. This led to a cost problem, however, and Porsche was unable to agree to McLaren's wishes and take a 50-percent financial stake in the project.

In November it was agreed that Mezger's department should devote the following months to drawing up a design study for a suitable engine, at a cost of a million German Marks.

"We then had an engine with about 98 percent of its features defined", comments Hans Mezger proudly, "and after Mansour Ojjeh and his TAG (Techniques d´Avantgarde) company took up the project and the money was there, we never looked back!"

By December 1982, when the TAG turbo engine was going through its first rig tests, the 'age of the turbo' had arrived on the motor racing circuits in a big way. Eight Grand Prix races had already been won by turbocharged cars, and one of these had only just missed capturing the championship title. A year later, the situation is even more self-evident, with twelve races out of sixteen going to turbocharged cars.

The McLaren with Porsche's TAG turbo engine was entered for the last three races of the season. By 1984 it is on the starting line with all its muscles flexing and raring to go. Niki Lauda and Alain Prost took it in turns to win twelve races for McLaren. At the end of the Formula 1 series, Lauda made it onto the world champion's podium by a bare half a point. It was Prost's turn in the two following years.

The turbocharged engines became more powerful with each successive season. In 1984, the race versions were developing 820 horsepower, the practice versions up to 870. By 1987 these values had shot up to 960 and 1,060 horsepower although the boost pressure had been reduced from the usual 5 to only 4 bar. The turbocharged cars were far superior to the naturally aspirated ones, although these were permitted a swept volume of 3.5 liters. Nevertheless, the era of the Porsche turbocharged engine in Formula 1 was drawing to a close. The sponsoring agreement with TAG expired, the financial boost, so to speak, was gone, and McLaren began to get its power from Honda-V6 engines, just as one might have expected.

3

Turbo-technology gave the Porsche 917/30 its wings. Its twelve cylinder engine developed more than 1,100 horsepower

When the turbocharger first appeared in the nineteen-sixties, the messages it conveyed to the sporting automobile world still lacked the last quantum of conviction. The short but mercurial career of the Chevrolet Corvair Turbo seems not to have communicated an optimistic picture of this new technology to Porsche's forward thinkers. Doubtless the factory in Zuffenhausen studied the Chevrolet with its air-cooled flat-six rear engine very closely in the years in which they were developing a turbocharged version of their own 911, but this American creation produced no more than 150 horsepower from a displacement of 2.7 liters, peaking in 1966 at 180 horsepower.

Michael May's work on the Ford V6 engine yielded similar results: 180 horsepower, admittedly, from only 2.3 liters, but with a power curve that was in all honesty more of a steep straight-line gradient. May's engines perform devilishly well in the upper speed range, but lack an equivalent amount of pulling power at lower engine speeds: with a four-speed gearbox, the result is an unsuitable partnership.

Yet soon there were new rumors emerging from the USA about the miracles performed by the turbocharger. On the Indianapolis oval and similar racetracks in that country, turbocharged Offenhauser four-cylinder engines with a displacement of 2.65 liters were producing vast amounts of power: in qualifying sessions 800, rising before very long to more than 1,000 horsepower.

The lap times grew shorter, but soon the word went around that it was only on such oval racetracks that the turbocharged engine was invincible, that it called for a very unusual driving technique that wouldn't work elsewhere. Very large turbochargers take an eternity to build up their boost pressure, which then has to be maintained so that a good lap time results. The right foot had to be rammed down on the gas pedal and kept there, the left foot was then used to brake the car sufficiently at the end of

OPEN-ENDED THRUST

The thousand-horsepower drive: track testing the Porsche 917/30

By Clauspeter Becker

the straights. The new technique from America was clearly unsuitable for any of Europe's racing circuits — a verdict of three to nil against the turbo, or so it seemed.

Be that as it may, Porsche went ahead with trials of a turbocharged version of the 911 flat-six engine, and as many people expected, the reports from the test rig confirmed that little progress was being made. Porsche therefore started a hunt for more power, of the magnitude needed to win the Le Mans 24-hour race, and in the latter half of the 1960s made a few significant steps forward along more orthodox lines.

Ferdinand Piëch, in his capacity as motor-sport and development departmental manager, put his faith in the traditional source of power: more swept volume. He instructed his team to start work on a twelve-cylinder engine, the Type 917, that would increase the capacity of the existing eight-cylinder unit from three to four and a half liters. The advantage of this linear development was that well-proven components could remain in use. The air-cooled cylinders retained the same bore and stroke, and only a few modifications were needed to the cylinder heads, which were also air-cooled. Two overhead camshafts on each cylinder bank operated two valves per combustion chamber — 24 in all, in other words no more than the modern six-cylinder production engine possesses.

The engine's underpinnings were distinctly more complex. Power take-off from the crankshaft was no longer at one end, but by gearwheels in the center, with a shaft leading to the clutch. The crankshaft

Chapter 3

throws were also different: the crankpins were wider, with two conrods acting on each of them. This in turn helped to reduce the length of the twelve-cylinder engine, a design not otherwise noted for its compact dimensions. It also meant a departure from the to-and-from principle of what the Germans call the 'boxer' engine. The Porsche 917, according to the strict technical definition, is a '180-degree V12' – though there is surely something contradictory in any language about a V with an included angle of 180 degrees.

After its roadholding had been successfully tamed, the Porsche 917 soon began to win one race after another: in 1970 the long-awaited victory in the Le Mans 24-hour event, in 1971 a repeat of this success. At the same time, the 917 found itself in the forefront of a horsepower escalation process that also led to Ferrari and Ford developing cars capable of exceeding 400 km/h (almost 250 mph) down the Mulsanne straight in Le Mans. As expected, the rules had to be changed, and from then on only three-liter engines were permitted.

This left the Porsche competition department with an out-of-work race winner. As the season wore on, it was also evident that a 917 in its original form had very little chance of success in the American CanAm series either. Swiss driver Jo Siffert took it to the start there for Audi-Porsche, but without any real prospects of defeating the McLaren with its eight-liter V8 Chevrolet engine.

24 25 *In 1973 the Porsche 917/30 was unbeatable: it won every race in the CanAm Series and brought Mark Donohue the champion's title*

In the cockpit of Mark Donohue's 917/30: efficient engineering predominates over styling

26 *The 917/30's tires had 1,100 horsepower to transmit as well as a thousand Newton-meters of torque or even more*

For success in CanAm racing, two strategies were worked out initially. The first was in favor of a much larger 16-cylinder engine with a displacement of 6.5 liters and a power output of 755 hp. Before long, though, another approach proved to be far more promising, and in 1971 the Porsche Competition Department decided to look more closely into the advantages offered by the turbocharger.

Motor expert Hans Mezger recalls: "This was a suggestion made by Ferdinand Piëch shortly before he left our company. We only took it up after we had already won Le Mans twice. That's the way it always was: first of all we concentrated all our efforts on Le Mans, after that we started to look at new projects."

Before getting too deeply involved in turbocharger technology, Porsche's technicians asked themselves a very sensible question: "Where did all the others go wrong?"

Analysis of the situation suggested that the combination of a relatively large turbocharger with a waste gate in the pressure line leading to the inlet valves as a means of blowing off excess boost was fundamentally wrong, since it could only supply peak power, nothing further down the scale – and was in any case poorer in its overall efficiency. The better alternative, Porsche's technical experts felt, would be a smaller charger that could build up plenty of boost at lower speeds of rotation and persuade the engine to deliver more power at lower revs. This concept was all well and good, but it meant modifying and improving the boost pressure control principle. Porsche's engineers were the first to hit upon the

28

Chapter 3

idea of supplying only as much exhaust gas to the turbine as it needed to create the maximum boost pressure. They then needed a valve on the hot side of the system to discharge the excess exhaust gas to atmosphere. After some experimenting with flap valves, they found a modified version of the classic exhaust valve to be the best answer – and in suitably developed form, such a device is now performing well on many millions of turbocharged engines everywhere.

With this brilliant device taking care of the boost control problem, the way was clear for the CanAm engine to be completed without delay. Even a turbocharged engine, it was felt, could only benefit from a little extra swept volume, and the 917/10 was therefore powered by a version with a capacity of five liters. At a boost pressure of 1.4 to 1.5 bar, the result was 1,000 hp at 7,800 rpm, with a peak torque of 981 Newton-meters at 6,400 rpm.

For the CanAm races, the rules called for this potent twelve-cylinder engine to be housed in a (theoretically) open two-seater body with right-hand drive. The car's basic engineering was conservative: the 917/10 inherited the light alloy lattice-tube frame from its predecessor, although by now the era of monocoque body construction had arrived. The frame for the new CanAm car was built from magnesium, but the critical Roger Penske evidently found it insufficiently attractive, and had the cars disassembled again and the frame polished all over.

Sports car bodies are styled, if at all, in the wind tunnel. The development target is not merely minimum drag but also maximum downforce. None the less, it still comes as a surprise to learn that in 1972

32

33

The carbon-fiber era hadn't yet begun when these massive glass-fiber reinforced epoxy resin body elements for the 917/30 were produced

30 Only on the first lap was the field as close together as this in Riverside,
31 during a 1973 CanAm race. Donohue and Follmer usually established an early lead on their way to yet another victory

the 917/10 had the astronomically high aerodynamic drag coefficient of $c_D = 0.65$, and that a year later the equivalent figure for the longer-bodied 917/30 was still 0.60.

The American Roger Penske entered the two Porsche 917/10s with Mark Donohue and George Follmer as their drivers. He managed the team with technical support from the manufacturer's racing department, and a 'striking' success, if this description can be allowed, was achieved the first time out at Mosport in Canada. Mark Donohue caused some anxiety at first by returning to the pit and complaining about lack of power. Mechanic Valentin Schäffer diagnozed this as pressure escaping through a relief valve in the fresh mixture line that was intended only to operate in an emergency. When Hans Mezger tells the story today, one can sense some of the horror with which he saw Valentin seize a hammer and strike the valve a few resounding blows until it consented to behave itself. After this excitement, Donohue managed a very respectable second place. Later, however, the Porsches were more than a match for the classic CanAm cars: from mid-season on they began to defeat the McLarens, the Lolas and the Shadows, and at the end of October it was George Follmer who beamed down from the winner's podium, since star driver Donahue was still recovering from an accident during testing.

In 1973 Porsche and Penske started the CanAm season with the same drivers, but with two new cars. To handle the extra power, the wheelbase was lengthened. The 917/30 has a displacement of 5.4 liters and a power output officially quoted as 1,100 hp at 7,800 rpm. This was clearly only a maximum value dictated by safety factors. Hans Mezger well remembers a by-pass valve sticking during a test-rig run, so that boost pressure was no longer limited: "By the time we were able to shut the engine down, it was delivering somewhere between 1,400 and 1,500 horsepower. It didn't come to any harm, either!" There are no records of the torque that the engine was developing at this stage in the session, but even the officially noted figure is awe-inspiring enough: 1,098 Newton-meters at 6,400 rpm. Cooling an engine such as this was a hard task for the centrally mounted fan: 3,100 liters of air a second are needed to keep the temperature down to a reasonable level. None of the engines had a charge-air intercooler as a source of extra power, and Hans Mezger is perfectly ready to admit: "We didn't need one, we had far too much power already!"

With this more than healthy engine output, the Porsche 917 completed the 1972 and 1973 seasons with a four-speed gearbox. Traction problems attributable to the sheer abundance of power were dealt with by radical methods. The 917/30 had no rear-axle differential all, only a rigid final drive. This performed admirably in the actual races, but the mechanics found the cars rather difficult to maneuver at slow speeds in the pits or the paddock, despite their surprisingly slim outlines of a 1,100-hp car with a dry weight of only 800 kilograms (1,765 lbs). On the starting line, admittedly, the 917/30 weighed in at about a ton, since its considerable thirst, sometimes as severe as one liter per kilometer, called for a 400-liter (106 gallon) fuel tank to be accommodated and filled to the brim.

Mark Donohue, the racing driver and graduate engineer, played a major part in the development of the 917/10 and 917/30, and their subsequent success. He had a brilliant career that took him in due course into Formula 1, but ended tragically with a fatal accident in Zeltweg during the Austrian Grand Prix

In the 1973 CanAm series, the Porsche 917/30 proved to be more in command of the situation than ever. Penske's "German Tanks" carried all before them and won every single race in the series. After a season driven without the slightest error, Donohue took the championship title ahead of Follmer.

Nevertheless, the turbocharged cars' days were numbered. The first oil crisis cast its shadow over all kinds of motor sport. As a precaution, the 1974 CanAm series was run under new rules that prohibited the turbocharged juggernauts entirely. Since then the series has lost its worldwide reputation.

In 1975, Mark Donohue took his pensioned-off title-winning car out onto America's fastest oval racetrack in Talladega, Alabama, in an attempt to break a few records. No sooner said than done: his fastest lap of the 4.28-kilometer (2.66-mile) track was 37.3 seconds, an average speed of 355.848 km/h (221.1 mph) – the highest lap speed achieved on any racetrack until then. Donohue's top speed on the straight was timed at 413.6 km/h (257 mph). For these record runs the 917/30's body was suitably modified and the engine given a charge-air intercooler that boosted its power yet again quite considerably.

4

On Germany's 'autobahns', which have no blanket speed limit, the only restrictions on the Turbo with a skilled person at the wheel are the other traffic and how far the driver can see.

From the Swiss periodical 'Automobil Revue', 1975

THE POWER THAT CAME OUT OF THE CRISIS

By Clauspeter Becker, with quotations from auto motor und sport, Automobil Revue and Road & Track

How the Porsche Turbo appeared in 1974 to buck the automobile-industry trend sparked off by the first oil crisis – and what it was like to drive a Porsche Turbo 25 years ago

A look at the expert views that accompanied the Turbo into an era that was afterwards named for this pioneering car.

The enthusiasm felt by the 1975 authors can be sensed between the lines of their test reports. Yet optimism was in short supply that year in the automobile industry. The oil crisis was a healthy shock, or at least that was the euphemism often used for it.

The world was still reeling under this shock when the Porsche Turbo burst onto the scene. A milestone – and all three articles quoted from here confirm the authors' respect for the manufacturer's achievement.

The test team from the Swiss publication **Automobil Revue** identified the Turbo correctly as one of those pioneer acts that usher in a new era in automobile construction.

In the American magazine **Road & Track** Joe Rusz got to the roots of the car's long period of success: "The Turbo is the fastest and the most civilized Porsche ever built!"

Last but not least, Gert Hack in **auto motor und sport** writes with great diplomacy, in the face of the blanket speed-limit threat: "Not only can the Turbo be driven slowly, it can even be fun to do so!"

From the brief test in the Swiss
AUTOMOBIL REVUE
magazine dated August 21, 1975

THERE IS UNLIKELY TO BE unanimity among the general public about this remarkable car. In view of its appearance, many critical observers will dismiss it as a sports car with an unnecessarily powerful engine; others will see its successful use of turbocharging as a landmark in technical progress, still others will regard it as an example of the absolute elite in international high-performance car design, but one that is nevertheless suitable for day-to-day driving.

There may be some truth in all these views, since they are backed by hard facts: this is an exceptionally luxurious, well-equipped model (as indeed it should be for a selling price of 78,650 Swiss francs)! But it is also capable of being used in a perfectly normal way on our roads.

The source of this car's overwhelming power is the turbocharger, a device driven by the exhaust gas leaving the engine and originally developed by the late Alfred Büchi, a Swiss engineer, who applied it to large diesel engines many years ago and obtained much more power as well as improved economy from them.

Until now the turbocharger has seldom been applied to production cars (with the exception of the Chevrolet Corvair Corsa from 1965 to 1966 and the BMW 2002 Turbo from 1973 to 1974), though some tuning companies have offered it as add-on equipment. The turbocharger has been more widespread in racing car design, especially in the USA, and Porsche's work on it has been exceptionally successful.

Chapter 4

Handling the Turbo is something that needs to be learned. Since the clutch bites instantly, the newcomer's first efforts to drive off may end with a stalled engine. But slightly more gas and a mild amount of clutch slip will yield the desired forward movement, and as soon as the road is clear you can put your foot down harder.

Nothing that could be described as awe-inspiring happens at first, but when the crucial engine speed of 3,700 rpm is reached (45, 78, 114 and 156 km/h or 28, 49, 71 and 97 mph in the four gears), the power comes in strongly and catapults the car forward in a way that even surprises an 'old AR test hand'.

Our top speed of 246 km/h (152.8 mph) failed to match Porsche claim of 250 km/h (155.3 mph), but that is surely academic. Among todays high-performance cars only the Ferrari BB, the Lamborghini Countach and the Hai (Shark), the latter built to special order only, perform equally well or better. Porsche's Carrera 3.0 actually reaches the 100 km/h (62 mph) mark from a standing start just before the Turbo, but by the time 120 km/h (75 mph) comes up it is already being left behind.

Is it a landmark, an unnecessary development or maybe a peak engineering achievement? If you regard every automobile as a basically banal mode of transport, you'll shake your head in despair about the Turbo. But if you understand the urge to explore the limit in every area, you may well recognize the true pioneering value of this turbocharged car, which seems without exaggeration to have been "born a classic".

On such German 'autobahns' as have no speed limit at all, a Turbo with a skilled driver at the wheel encounters no obstacles at all apart from other vehicles and the visibility limit. But the driver's capabilities are none the less important, since it is all too easy to underestimate the Turbo's speed. The turbocharger reduces exhaust noise and the well-built body causes very little wind roar. At 200 km/h (125 mph) you can listen to the radio without difficulty.

Anyone who travels by Turbo on the German highway should therefore keep an eagle eye open for speed-limit signs, and watch the speedometer especially closely when turning off onto ordinary main roads.

The 'AR' test team

For ROAD & TRACK

Joe Rusz described the Turbo as follows

Unlike other versions of the 911, the Turbo Carrera is easy to spot. Huge, bulbous fenders (part of its RSR legacy), protrude visibly from the sides of the car and conceal wheels and tires (7-in. front, 8-in. rear) that strangely enough are also used on the more conventionally bodied '75 Carrera. The Turbo uses the familiar whale-tail rear spoiler and the rubber-edged front spoiler both of which appeared on last year's model. Thankfully, the garish Carrera side lettering is gone and only a patch of black script lettering mounted on the rear deck lid (under the whale tail) indicates that this is a Turbo Carrera. Special paint and headlight washers serve as additional reminders.

Porsche's heavy artillery for '76 is the Turbo Carrera, a dazzingly fast road car that shares a common heritage with Porsche racing cars of the last few seasons. Its body and suspension are spinoffs from the Group 4 RSR, while its engine is a detuned version of the Group 5 racing turbo powerplant. Yet in spite of a heavy infusion of racing blood, the Turbo Carrera road car is easily the fastest and most civilized 911 ever built.

Top speed is a respectable 155 mph, while 0-60 mph acceleration times are in the 5- to 6-sec bracket. Unfortunately, the Turbo's top speed is commensurate with its price. Both are high, meaning the 400-or-so lucky 1976 U.S. buyers will have to pay about $26,000 for their very own Turbo.

Exhaust emissions are controlled by an air injection pump and thermal reactor combination that along with retarded ignition timing makes the Turbo legal in all 50 states, but also robs it of 16 bhp compared to the European engine. Not to worry, because the difference in the two models' performance is minimal.

Joe Rusz

Gert Hack wrote about the 'Driving Force' in auto motor und sport

It was in October 1974 that Porsche showed its top 'turbo' model at the Paris Motor Show. This was at a time when the entire German automobile industry and in particular the Zuffenhausen-based sports car manufacturer Porsche was still suffering from the after-effects of a recession. It was also a time when small, economical cars were attracting much more interest than exclusive models with powerful engines.

So was Porsche backing the wrong horse? Wouldn't it have been mich better to develop a smaller-engined, less powerful version of the 911 with a less opulently equipped and trimmed interior? The answer is no. The future of a sports car manufacturer like Porsche and indeed its only reason for continuing to exist is to pursue technical progress and give its cars exclusive character – an economy model just wouldn't fit into the picture. What more logical response, therefore, than to compensate at least partly for a drop in sales income by launching a more expensive model at the top of the range?

And so this top-performing, exclusive Porsche was introduced ...

... with its turbocharged engine, Porsche in fact achieved two things at once: the desired increase in power and also a further gain in prestige and exclusive technical character. The idea of selling a turbocharged production car was tempting in view of Porsche's success for some years with competition 911 engines of this type; it is doubtful whether any other manufacturer had as much practical experience of turbocharging as Porsche at that time.

Chapter 4

The Porsche turbo isn't a racing car in disguise – you become aware of this the moment you turn the ignition key. The powerful engine at the back starts to rumble contentedly and reliably, whether it was cold or already warm. Even if you push the gas pedal down sharply, you hear nothing from the exhaust apart from the usual Porsche sound – on this car, rather more strongly damped than on other Porsches.

You can drive off without any difficulty and cruise around at low engine speeds – 2,000 rpm or even lower in fourth gear. The engine doesn't take offense. You see: driving the 'turbo' slowly isn't merely possible, it can even be fun!

Agreed, the enjoyment perks up rapidly when you find yourself on a clear stretch of road. The acceleration is then not far removed from what a racing car would offer. You reach 80 km/h (50 mph) in first gear after only 3.6 seconds, by the time you're at 140 km/h (87 mph) it's time to get into third gear, and the 'turbo' hurtles you past the 200 km/h (125 mph) mark in under 20 seconds. It's as if its flow of power is inexhaustible.

Gert Hack

... the device that makes this engine so interesting, the turbocharger, is concealed from inquisitive eyes. The only way to see it is to get under the 'turbo' and look upward. There it is – quite small, flanged to the muffler on the left side of the engine.

Porsche has reduced the typical shortcoming of the turbocharged engine, its delayed response to the throttle, to a minimum on this car. You only notice it when you put your foot down after a corner or when accelerating from a moderate engine speed at part load. It's something you very soon get accustomed to. However, taking corners in a continuous drift becomes more or less impossible. The 'turbo' driver should therefore choose the 'Mark Donohue method': enter the corner relatively slowly and accelerate out hard. Thanks to wide tires and a high driven-axle load, the 'turbo' puts its power on the ground very effectively, so that this cornering method brings good results.

... step on the gas, a terrifyingly powerful 'turbo thrust' builds up suddenly and the car shoots forward like a rocket with the rear wheels skittering over the track surface

Chapter 5

YOUR OWN PAST VANISHES FIRST FROM THE MEMORY: what exactly did happen twenty years or more ago? It's lost in the mists of the mind, the contours have become vague. Many weeks, even months, of our lives then are gone from the memory, whereas other events can be recalled to mind in dramatic colors as if they had only happened a few days ago.

That's how I remember making the acquaintance of the Porsche 934 Turbo. It was at the racetrack in Hockenheim, during the six-hour event that was one of the heats of the constructors' world championship. I couldn't have been warned more emphatically: "This car is a brute – you have to watch it like a hawk!" said Edgar Dören, whose co-driver I was in the Valvoline 934 for this race. Manfred Schurti took me aside then and said: "It's not as bad as that! But keep the throttle open when you're braking, so that the boost pressure builds up. And brake early – the car is heavy!" As an amateur race driver, I had no trouble at all in following this last bit of advice. I remember that in practice I bore down on ther East Curve at a healthy tempo.

In those days there wasn't a chicane and most cars could take the corner at between 180 and 200 kilometers an hour (110 to 125 miles an hour). Before I reached the 300-meter board I was thinking hard about the fancy footwork that was about to be called for: release the clutch with the left foot, press the brake pedal with the right toe and pump the throttle with the right heel, to avoid losing boost pressure. I have never forgotten what happened next. Just as I was concentrating wholeheartedly on my feet, Manfred Winkelhock shot past to my right in the Group 5 BMW 320, a car that weighed eight hundredweight less although it had a less powerful engine. He still has his foot hard down on the gas pedal!

A VERY MILD EXPRESSION OF POWER

By Eckhard Schimpf

Remember how it was in 1976, when a Porsche 934 that looked almost standard weighed 800 kilograms and had 500 horsepower to move them?

Through the open side window the noise of a screaming four-valve engine revolving at about ten thousand revs a minute was genuinely painful. A moment later, Winkelhock's brake lights finally came on, then it was time for me to take the corner as well. I put my right foot down again when I reached the peak of the curve, and the massive thrust of the turbocharged engine was still there! The tail of the car skittered about as it shot forward like a rocket into the Motodrome.

Just a minor episode, a scrap of memory that has floated to the surface. But it reminded me all too clearly of the problems associated with the 934 Turbo. This product of Porsche's competition department first appeared on the starting grid in 1976, and in the first phase of its career at least, struck terror into most of its drivers. For good reason.

The FISA drew up new race rules for 1976. The constructors' world championship that the public had always loved so much and which was very close to Formula 1 in its appeal was now to be contested by Group 5 cars, not the previous open sports cars, and there were also changes in the rules for GT cars. At Porsche, the era of normally aspirated engines had come to an end in 1974 and 1975, with the truly outstanding Carrera RSR (three liters capacity, 330 horsepower). The new Gran Turismo cars were based on the Porsche 930, with a turbocharged engine. This was why the racing version became the Type 934, with the 4 reminding us that

Chapter 5

according to the international federation these were Group 4 cars (in the same way, the Group 5 Porsche was known as the Type 935). This was the first time an 'equivalent' formula had been arrived at. Wheel width was limited to 14 inches and rim width to 12.5 inches. These BBS magnesium wheels were rather narrow, compared with the previous year's massively shod RSR. Another problem was the rear wing, that had to be kept very small, as on the basic model, and in the engine-size category up to 4 liters a minimum weight of 1,120 kilograms (2,470 lbs) was therefore laid down. As a result of this, no excessive weight-saving measures had to be applied to the 934's bodyshell. These turbocharged GTs were accordingly some of the most luxuriously equipped cars ever to take to the track. They had electric window lifts just like the standard model, and when they were delivered the cigarette lighter was actually still in place and working, to everyone's surprise.

At that time, the Porsche 934 cost 97,000 German Marks. About 30 were built, and sold to leading racing teams (Kremer, Loos etc.) and private entrants. The engine had a compression ratio of 6.5:1 and K-Jetronic fuel injection for the first time. Its initial output, running a boost pressure of 1.4 bar, was 480 hp at 7,000 rpm. Later the boost was upped to 1.6 bar in some cases and engine allegedly delivered 560 or even 580 horsepower. Since the car was relatively narrow, the aerodynamics were good and well over 300 km/h (185 mph) could be seen on the speedometer. In short: plenty of power, but narrow tires, high weight and the assorted teething troubles associated with the early days of turbocharging. Not surprising, that the 934 was regarded as a nervous racing car and was not greatly loved (compared, say, with the Carrera RSR).

Helmut Kelleners was one of the drivers who took up the challenge offered by the 934 in those days. His comment, looking back: "It was a highly critical box of tricks. Particularly at the Nürburg Ring. Brutally fast, with very little downforce, not a car you could slide easily." Other ace drivers of the day such as Bob Wollek,

48 *June 27, 1976 at the Noris Ring: Reinhard Stenzel at the wheel of the Max Moritz Porsche with start number 4.*
49 *The race was won by Bob Wollek with Stenzel second across the line*

Left: The Max Moritz 'armada' on the Diepholz airfield circuit in 1976. Kelleners, in front here, came in third overall.
At the right and on the next page (left): pit stops during the Nürburg Ring 1,000-kilometer race.
The 934s bearing the numbers 24 (driven by Kelleners and Stenzel) and 25 (driven by Bell and Steckkönig) came in third and tenth

Toine Hezemans, Tim Schenken and Reinhard Stenzel also took a cautious view of this fire-spitting wagon as the 1976 season drew closer. The Eifel Race on the Nürburg Ring was the first round in the German Sports Car Racing Championship and the first chance to come to grips with this car. Helmut Kelleners was the winner, the driver who tamed it more quickly than the others. He found the most suitable settings and – a specialty of his – completed the race with a lower fuel consumption and less brake pad wear than his rivals. This approach paid off, but later in the season, and after rolling the car badly in Mainz-Finthen, Kelleners was unable to score any more wins. Hezemans, Schenken and Wollek shared the remaining championship victories among themselves.

In the races for the 1976 manufacturers' world championship, and in 1977 and 1978 too, the 934 Turbo always performed well. Although there was only one overall win (Heimrath/Miller in the Mosport (Canada) 6-hour race in 1977), the cars were always among the first ten in the overall category that was dominated at that time by the Porsche 935 works cars (driven by Ickx, Mass, Stommelen and Schurti) and the BMW CSL competition cars.

This was the also picture at the 1,000-kilometer race on the Nürburg Ring in 1976. The Jägermeister Max-Moritz team had entered two 934s (with Derek Bell, Kelleners, Steckkönig and Stenzel taking turns at the wheel) and a naturally aspirated RSR, which I drove together with Edgar Dören. I remember that during the final practice session Max-Moritz team manager Rudi Sauter asked Bell to 'bed down' the brakes of our RSR. He came back to the pit and said: "I'd far sooner be driving your car without the turbo. It handles marvelously. These 934s are a bit of shit. This is a miserable job. And having to drive two cars as well ... ." Derek began to think aloud: "It'll be tough tomorrow. I usually drive straight back to England after the race. But I won't be able to do that tomorrow. I'll be too worn out! I'd better stay here till Monday!"

This 1,000-kilometer race wasn't just tough for Derek Bell, who had to wrestle almost uninterruptedly

In the manufacturers' world championship the turbocharged cars from Stuttgart dominated the GT class until the early 1980s

A '934 and a half', in other words a Porsche 934 with extra-wide tires, flared fenders and a bigger rear wing for Group 5 racing. This is Edgar Dören at the Nürburg Ring in 1977

Chapter 5

with one of the two Max-Moritz cars; it was also an impressive demonstration of what the 934s could do. After Rolf Stommelen retired the factory-entered 935, overall victory went to a BMW (Quester/Krebs), but it was followed by a string of 934s in places two to six: Hezemans/Schenken, Bell/Kelleners/Stenzel, then Haldi/Hotz, van Lennep/Bertrams and Bross/Sindel. I came in seventh with Dören in the naturally-aspirated RSR, which also took the class win in Group 5 for cars up to three liters, and still more 934s followed us across the line, including the second Max-Moritz car driven by Stenzel/Steckkönig/Bell, which was tenth.

After this, the Porsche 934 remained a powerful tool in the hands of private entrants for several years. The red-hot turbochargers and the retirements they caused in the 1976 season were increasingly infrequent. In the events counting toward the manufacturers' world championship, the turbocharged cars from Stuttgart dominated the GT category until the early 1980s. Toine Hezemans was GT world champion in 1976, and in Le Mans the 934s won the GT class in the 24-hour race several times. French driver Jacques Almeras picked up the European hillclimb championship and in 1978 Angelo Pallavicini from Switzerland was in turn GT world cup winner (just ahead of Edgar Dören) – a very impressive career for a racing car that the drivers had originally condemned as a 'brute'.

Edgar Dören again, this time hustling the 934 round the Noris Ring in 1977

The initial plan for the Porsche to end all Porsches was formulated back in 1982

Chapter 6

1987 ISN'T SO VERY LONG AGO, but 420,000 German Marks was still a small fortune. It would have bought a decent house in a respectable area for the family, and paid for some new furniture as well. Whoever invested such a sum in motor vehicles could have opened a dealership the next day – it would have bought thirty VW Golfs. Alternatively, why not blow the whole sum on a single car, of which only two hundred were planned – the Porsche 959.

Anyone who suspected that with this healthy purchase price for the most elaborate version of the 911 ever built, Porsche was raking in the profits, was barking up the wrong tree. Helmuth Bott, then the company's Technical Director, made this quite clear when the Super-911 was introduced, even if it wasn't part of his public statement: "Our development costs have been so immense that if anything Porsche is making a loss on each of these cars."

The journalists' proverbially hard hearts bled, but at the same time they hit on a clear definition for the car that was about to become the high-tech icon of its time: the 959 was not only the latest dream car and technology leader, but at the same time the most expensive give-away the company had ever offered its well-heeled customers – hand-built from the floor pan upward in the Weissach racing department.

The initial plan for the Porsche to end all Porsches was formulated back in 1982, when the company's chief executive officer was Peter W. Schutz, an American. The four-, six- and eight-cylinder 944, 911 and 928 models were selling like hot cakes, and the new Type 956 competition car was dominating the prototypes in the major sports-car events such as Le Mans and Daytona.

WHEN THE PRESSURE IS ON

By Malte Jürgens

In a gripping three-act drama, Porsche harnessed the power of the multi-stage turbocharged engine for the 959

The business climate was good for a supersports car concept to be conceived and to germinate: Porsche would introduce a road model with state-of-the-art automobile technology under the skin in every possible design area. This would be a breathtaking reference model, a display of the finest in automobile engineering and tangible evidence of what the Weissach 'think tank' could produce when given a free hand.

Project leader Manfred Bantle consulted the competition rules issued by the FIA, the international automobile sport federation, before sketching out the 959 for the first time. Although it was intended to be a roadgoing car, it was none the less a genuine Porsche in the sense of putting up a convincing performance on the racetrack too – in Group B, which was to be the future category for the world sports car championship. There was no lack of awe-inspiring competitors: even Ferrari was planning to send its 288 GTO, and later the F 40, to the starting line and contend for this hotly contested championship trophy.

This determined the minimum number of 959s that would have to be built: Group 2 rules called for 200 identical cars.

On January 21, 1983 Bantle was instructed by technical director Bott to start work on a Group B design study, and scarcely a week later, the first sketches were on the table.

Attempts to use the 944 or 928 as a basis failed to yield very promising results, and so the 911 was chosen as the starting point. The internal requirement specification described what can only be called a 'domesticated racing car', with an initial power output somewhere between 400 and 500 horsepower, aerodynamics suitable for racing speeds – and an advanced form of four-wheel drive. Helmuth Bott had a number of reasons for departing from Porsche's typical rear-wheel-drive layout: "There are four factors we have to harmonize: the best possible road-holding, perfect handling, stability in a straight line and of course optimum power distribution to each of the four wheels."

The 959, initially known within the company as the 911 Group B car or the F3 project, was on its way, with an unrivalled concept. Porsche was about to create a well-appointed GT car with an unbelievable amount of power on tap, that not only stood a good chance of making it to the winners' podium in sports-car races but would even turn in a good performance off-road if suitably modified.

Jacky Ickx, the retired Formula 1 driver, persuaded the company to take part in the Paris-Dakar Rally, an event much feared for the rough treatment it meets out to participating vehicles. Porsche agreed to provide the Ickx team with experimental cars based on the Type 930, reduced in weight, with raised suspension – and with a great many of the forthcoming 959's technical features under the skin.

Unbelievable, but true: more or less on its first outing, Porsche won the world's toughest rally with this car. Even more astonishing: winning driver René Metge in the 959 prototype was followed across the finishing line by experimental engineer Roland Kussmaul, in an unconventional service car powered by a 928 engine. The secret of this remarkable achievement: he simply stayed close behind the winning car! In 1986 Metge repeated Porsche's triumph and confirmed the merits of the 959's technical features even before the

56

For the highway, the racetrack and the tree-lined country road: the 959 looks good and performs well everywhere

54 *High-tech in a restrained package: Porsche's most potent model conceals*
55 *its horsepower under a smooth exterior*

The sport seats have plenty of body location; not much can be seen of the engine apart from its cooling fan

car's official launch was due. An impressive baptism in the hot sand of the Sahara Desert and a brilliant run-up to the appearance of the production car.

What was the secret of the technical supremacy that this athlete from the Zuffenhausen factory so obviously possessed? The obvious place to look is the power train. The 959 has its engine at the back, in the best 911 tradition. Ahead of it are the clutch housing and the rear-axle final drive with its differential. Flanged to this is an all-synchromesh gearbox with rod-operated manual shift, six forward ratios and reverse. From the front of this gearbox a steel propeller shaft runs forward in a central tube to drive the front wheels.

A new, high-tech design feature avoids the need for a centre differential to equalize the front- and rear-axle rotating speeds: Porsche's controlled clutch, or PSK for short, acts on both axles.

Its central element is a pack of 13 clutch disks, pressed together with a varying degree of force by an electronically-controlled hydraulic system to yield a form of controlled slip. This device is capable of distributing varying amounts of engine torque to the two axles. If both rear wheels have plenty of grip, all the power goes to them. But if wheelspin sets in, the PSK system gradually diverts power away and sends it to the front wheels instead, until a 50:50 percent torque split is reached.

Another function of the controlled clutch is to lock the rear differential by any value up to the full 100 percent, so that wheelspin can be counteracted as soon as it starts and optimum traction is available in any cir-

58

cumstances, just as in a thoroughbred racing car. In practice, the system operates along the following lines: if the wheel sensors installed for the anti-lock braking system indicate that one rear wheel is beginning to spin, a command is sent to the rear differential to activate the lock. If the entire axle still suffers from excessive wheelspin, the controlled clutch between the axles goes into action as we have already described, and redistributes the engine's torque.

The 959's driver has only to choose between four computer programs that set the PSK system to suit the prevailing road conditions: dry road, wet road, ice and snow or maximum traction. After this, the computer varies the hydraulic control system's settings automatically.

What the 959 did not have, on the other hand, was any form of traction control that would use the drive-by-wire electronic gas pedal settings and the ABS system to control the car close to its handling limits. The engineers were of the opinion that such a restrictive system would not match the character of their dynamic new sports car, with the result that the 'super-turbo' can be steered with the throttle as it approaches the handling limit, in a manner that the founding fathers at Porsche would certainly have approved of.

Such stupendous performance calls for equally fine brakes. It would be an understatement to describe Porsche's way of bringing the 959 to a standstill as a mere braking system: it was the yardstick by which all other competitors were measured. The brake disks were of a pattern already proved in the Porsche 917 competition cars: internally ventilated and cross-drilled. The diameter of the front brake disks had never been seen before on a production car: 322 millimeters (12.7 inches). Those at the back were almost as large, at

This is not kind of 'mad dog': the 959 displays its sporting character in a very civilized way

304 millimeters (12 inches). The four-piston alloy calipers had pistons of different sizes to ensure that the large-area pads incurred an equal rate of wear.

The anti-lock braking system was another technical highlight. The engineers exerted all their skill to develop a system that could still identify individual locked wheels even with four-wheel-drive in action and the rear differential locked. Together with the Wabco-Westinghouse company they designed a four-channel ABS system capable of varying the braking pressure at each individual wheel. It employs a particularly high pulse rate so that changes in road-wheel rotating speed are identified very quickly. For safety reasons, the pulse signals are processed in parallel by two computers.

The 959's 17-inch wheels were another remarkable technical achievement. The first version used Denloc tires from the Dunlop company, based on a motor racing design and with a generous margin of safety in the event of pressure loss. A monitoring system displayed the tire pressures to the driver. The wheels had hollow cast spokes that contained the same air as the tires themselves, so that the system was also capable of confirming that the wheels were undamaged – a reassuring item of information in a sports car capable of speeds up to 300 km/h (186 mph) and beyond. The wheels were independently suspended on lateral control arms, and Porsche installed two spring and shock absorber struts at each wheel. Since this was the 959 and no lesser car, the shock absorber settings were electronically controlled.

Chapter 6

One of each pair of shock absorbers came from the Bilstein company and had an automatic adjustment system that responded to road-surface conditions. The driver too was able to select three basic settings: soft for maximum ride comfort, normal or firm for enthusiastic driving.

The second set of shock absorbers came from Fichtel & Sachs and included a hydraulic ride-height control facility. In the normal setting the 959 had a ground clearance of 120 millimeters (4.7 inches), but two raised settings could also be selected (150 mm/5.9 in and 180 mm/7.1 in). When the car reached a predetermined road speed, however, the suspension was automatically lowered again: above 80 km/h (50 mph) back to 150 millimeters and above 160 km/h (100 mph) back to the lowest setting.

So much for the high-tech trio consisting of suspension, brakes and four-wheel driveline – but where was the power to come from? When designing the 959's engine, Porsche delved into a number of parts bins containing race-proven motor sport components, and also developed a novel form of multi-stage turbocharging as a source of additional power. But just about every detail of this engine deserves a closer look.

There was no retreating from the demand that the 959 should be capable of putting up a convincing show on the world's motor-racing circuits. Clearly, it had to have the mechanical strength to withstand far higher power outputs and loads than would be encountered in regular road use.

Porsche therefore adopted the well-proven vertically split crankcase that had already demonstrated its powers of endurance in the competition versions of the company's 935, 936, 956 and 962 models at out-

In the 1990s the Porsche Turbo developed into a 450-horsepower car entirely suitable for day-to-day use

puts of up to 640 horsepower. The steel crankshaft of this horizontally opposed 'Boxer' engine revolves in seven main bearings, and the pistons are attached to six terrifyingly expensive titanium conrods.

The light alloy pistons run in air-cooled cylinders of the same material, with Nikasil-coated walls. A novel feature on any production Porsche at that time was the use of water-cooled cylinder heads, already successful on the competition cars. Four valves per cylinder were actuated by two chain-driven overhead camshafts per cylinder bank. Other affinities with the racing engines were the sodium-filled exhaust valves and the use of dry sump engine lubrication. Hydraulic valve clearance adjusters were provided.

The engine's bore and stroke were 95 x 67 millimeters, yielding a swept volume of 2.85 liters. When the turbocharging factor for Group B racing was applied, this put the 959 among the four-liter normally-aspirated cars – its designers considered this to be the most promising compromise between potential power output and the permitted weight limit.

Porsche's engine design team in Weissach, however, had another card up their sleeve: the unique multi-stage turbocharging principle. The 959 engine was equipped with two turbochargers supplied by KKK, of a type that had already proved extremely reliable in the 944 Turbo. But in contrast to other 'biturbo' systems they were not operated in parallel all the time, but initially in series. The advantage of this: the exhaust-driven turbine runs up more rapidly to its operating speed and the engine's throttle response is improved. As engine speed rises beyond 4,300 rpm, a valve opens and the second turbocharger runs up. As soon as its boost pressure reaches a useful level, another valve switches the turbochargers to parallel operation and they both deliver air at the boost pressure of 1.9 bar needed for good cylinder filling. If still higher boost pressures are reached, the waste gate opens electronically. Two massive charge air intercoolers located in the rear side panels of the body keep the intake air temperature low. Fuel injection and ignition are controlled by a new Bosch Type MP engine management system (M for Motronic, P standing for the German word for 'pressure'). This system obtains its data from the pressures measured between the throttle butterfly and the inlet valves, and has the advantage that there is unrestricted flow through the inlet ports.

Other parameters such as load, engine speed and boost pressure, in some cases networked, are added to the complex computing process that determines the correct injected fuel volume and ignition timing. This efficient management system made the 959 a 'clean' car, with efficient combustion and low fuel consumption. Its performance in this respect put it at the top of the environmental acceptability scale – a remarkable feat for a supersport model, but its specific values were more impressive than those achieved by the far less exotic models on the market.

Thanks to the two-stage turbocharging principle and its elaborate control system, the engineers in Weissach were able to make the 959 eminently 'drivable'. The six-cylinder engine had none of the undesirable temperament of a conventional turbocharged unit. Its designers were wont to say: "It feels like an eight-liter normally aspirated engine when you drive it!" – and when the car was tested by the media, journalists wholeheartedly agreed with this assessment.

The figures on paper have no chance of revealing the potent but at the same time sliky character of the 959's engine. Power output was 450 hp at 6,500 rpm, and the maximum torque 500 Newton-meters at 5,500 rpm. The 'biturbo' continued to pump out its power up to a crankshaft speed of 7,600 rpm, and it was not until 8,200 rpm were reached that the governor cut in to avoid the risk of mechanical damage.

What of the body, with its impressive drag coefficient of 0.31? Basically speaking it consisted of the pressed-steel 911 bodyshell, with substantial reinforced side members and an integral roll cage for added rigidity.

The aluminum front hood panel and doors were 57 percent lighter than the equivalent steel components. Most of the other outer body elements were made from a six-layer glass-fiber and aramid composite. Each set of Kevlar elements for the 959's body, on reaching its finished form, was placed in an autoclave for three hours at a temperature of 130 °C and a pressure of two bar, in order to stabilize the structure of the material. After this the parts were trimmed to exact size with a fine high-pressure water jet delivered from a hardened nozzle, and bonded to the remainder of the steel body structure with epoxy resin.

After finishing work at butt joints on the PU material, the body received a second coat of epoxy primer and then its finish, consisting of several coats of acrylic paint. This mixed construction principle yielded a body full of functional elegance and with an ideal ratio of low weight to high strength. The crash tests confirmed this very clearly: the Porsche 959 was able to protect its occupants far better than many other cars in the event of an accident.

When the first 959s reached the public highway, the public held its breath in amazement – and there was surprise and consternation in other circles as well.

René Metge and Claude Ballot-Lena, driving the racing version of the 959 under its new Type 961 designation, spurred the new car on to no mean effect at Le Mans: seventh in the overall ratings and winner of its class. A year later, the FIA abolished Group B racing, allegedly for safety reasons, and the Porsche 959 was no longer able to pit its strength against the Ferrari, the Bugatti EB 110 and the Jaguar XJ 220.

The 959's mystique did not suffer from the FIA's decision. Even with only a limited racing career behind it, this complex, high-performance 911 derivative was praised by experts as a technical milestone. Certainly one does it a grave injustice to label it 'the most expensive Porsche give-away of all time'!

7

There may well be limits on further performance hikes in the not too distant future

Chapter 7

THE GENERAL MOOD IN GERMANY during 1974 was far from cheerful. Although the national soccer team took the world championship during the summer, the oil crisis a year previously had placed a distinct damper on the average Federal German citizen's ardor, and anxiety about the future was the mood of the day. Acute fuel shortages for road vehicles in the previous winter and a succession of Sundays on which motorized traffic was largely prohibited were unpleasant memories of all too recent a character, and there was a strong feeling that another round of the same treatment could be impending.

Germany's immense faith in the automobile had acquired a few superficial cracks, and in response to the newly awakened and still tentative desire for economy the car industry began to launch one underpowered model after another. Large-engined, powerful models were offered at ridiculously low prices on the secondhand market.

Such was the climate in which Porsche took the daring step of redefining the classic sports car. Even within the company's corridors of power there were doubts as to whether the Turbo, of all models, would be able to look forward to a promising future.

Dr. Ernst Fuhrmann, the company's technical director, paid little heed to such protests. He favored the turbocharged version of the 911 although the next supersport Porsche model, the 928, was already nearing production. His view proved to be correct, even if he didn't always express it in the most politically correct manner. When one of his well-paid staff at the Weissach development center asked him

HERO OF A LONG-RUNNING SERIES

How the Porsche Turbo developed in a quarter of a century into the perfect 'business express'

By Clauspeter Becker

whoever would be able to afford such a car, he replied in his quiet, high voice: "I am the only person here who earns enough to afford this car, and you must therefore expect me to know what people in my income bracket would buy!"

When the first Turbo was presented to the public in the fall of 1974, it came as something of a shock, not only because of the 260-horsepower engine, which seemed a little out of tune with the times, but also because of the price tag of 65,800 German Marks. It was as expensive as two regular Porsche 911s or a Mercedes 450 SEL 6.9 – though less than a secondhand Boxster would cost today. At the time, rumor had it that the luxury of leather upholstery and trim was chosen instead of a cheaper version because 'only a short run of 500 cars' was planned.

This is precisely where the marketing department seems to have been consulting the wrong oracle. The expensive Turbo was an immediate success, with the first 500 sold more or less overnight. A second batch was therefore laid down, and with it the legal growth limit reached. Porsche had refrained from applying for a German general operating permit for this, its Type 930/50, since only a few were to be made. Individual inspection was a means of avoiding all this paperwork, but was limited to a thousand cars of any given type. In no time at all, however, almost 1,500 Turbos had left the factory.

Chapter 7

Even the manufacturer's cautious plan not to let its Turbo tiger loose on the American market yielded very soon to popular demand. A US version was soon under construction, though there were evident problems in keeping the exhaust emissions under control.

The Turbo, a car that questioned every traditional principle of modesty, started its career with performance figures that were in no way unduly spectacular. The three-litre engine used the same 95-millimeter bore and 70.4 -millimeter stroke as the flat six in the Carrera RS 3.0. But whereas the latter reached its peak output of 230 hp only at 6,200 rpm, the Turbo dispensed 260 horsepower with ease at only 5,500 rpm, and its maximum torque of 343 Newton-meters at 4000 rpm was also evidence of greatly increased, but still relatively civilized, performance potential.

For 1974, the top speed of 250 km/h (155 mph) claimed by the factory was highly respectable, and when it came to the acceleration time from 0 to 100 km/h (62 mph) the experts were inclined to turn a blind eye to the fact that the same value of 5.4 seconds had already been achieved by the lightweight Carrera RS 2.7.

A quarter of a century ago the first Porsche Turbo was a rough diamond typical of the era, and certainly not the polished high-tech product one might expect today. The impression of unrestrained power set in only when the engine had climbed out of a severe flat spot typical of an early turbocharged unit; with only a four speed gearbox, moreover, it was often difficult for the driver to 'keep it on the cam'. New suspension components such as aluminum rear control arms, a broader track and wider tires were

68

In 1977 the first 3.3-liter Turbo again raised the standards higher, with 300 hp and 412 Nm of torque. Inside the flared wheel arches the Pirelli P 7 tires were still of relatively modest format: 205/50 VR 15 at the front and 225/50 VR 15 at the rear

66 *The monumental rear spoiler that was to become the Porsche Turbo's trade mark was taken from the motor sport department's parts bin.*
67 *Its task is to reduce aerodynamic lift at the rear axle*

needed to tame the potent rear engine even slightly. The car's innate tendency to oversteer could still be brought to the fore by injudicious use of the throttle, but also by closing it too suddenly. Brakes with the same specification as the remaining 911 models of the time needed hefty legwork before full retardation was available; the Porsches were given a brake booster only in the following model year.

For most of its customers the Turbo was not a car to be driven at the limit all the time, but one with a seductive quantity of power in reserve, to be brought forth only when needed. In fact the styling probably tempted more potential customers to pull out their wallets than the temptation to drive at almost twice the recommended German speed limit. To drive in a car with such curvaceous side panels is to flex one's muscles in a more subtile way. Within the flared wheel arches an advanced new type of low aspect-ratio tire held sway: the Pirelli P 7, with size 225/50 VR 15 at the rear wheels. The modern driver might well exclaim: Is that all?

The opulent lines of the widened body demanded a financial tribute, though at a time when 250 kilometers an hour was still an awe-inspiring challenge, it was of no fundamental significance. By 1963 standards, the aerodynamics of the original 911 were very good, but two factors now combined to worsen them: the car's broad cheeks increased its frontal area, and the sweeping curves caused the drag coefficient to deteriorate too, from $c_D = 0.36$ to 0.4. For these visual delights and the engine's extra power

70

output, customers were obliged to dig deeper into their pockets at the gas station. Of course, the 20 liters or so that the Turbo consumed every 100 kilometers (only 12 miles per US gallon) didn't break the bank entirely at 1973 fuel prices.

The success of the first Turbo committed Porsche's engineering team to develop a second version, to be even more perfect if such a thing was possible. The new version appeared in what one can only describe as 'turbo tempo'. In 1977 the new 300-hp car was to be seen at the German Motor Show in Frankfurt, and production began punctually in the fall, at the start of the 1978 model year.

The six-cylinder engine was 'bored and stroked', and now displaced 3,299 cc from a bore of 97 and a stroke of 74.4 millimeters. The power hike was far greater than the increased engine size suggested, thanks to the charge-air intercoolers located under the enlarged rear wing – the first time this device had been applied to a production car. Output went up to 300 hp and torque to 412 Nm, available as before at 4,000 rpm. This being 1978, the new model was designed to run on super-grade 98-octane gasoline containing lead. In the USA, Canada and Japan, where a lower octane number and unleaded fuel were already widespread, the power output suffered accordingly, having to be reduced to 265 hp.

The top speed was announced cautiously as 260 km/h (162 mph) and, since the new Turbo was a distinctly weightier car, the acceleration figures remained the same. The four-speed gearbox with its ratios chosen to make full use of the available torque was also retained – not ideal, but in view of the latest turbocharge engine's smooth pulling power an acceptable compromise.

In its character the Turbo that first appeared a quarter of a century ago was a rough diamond, not the polished high-tech product we would expect today

There was definite progress in the braking area: 17-inch wheels permitted brakes of larger size, with ventilated, drilled disks at front and rear and brake calipers derived directly from those used on the 1,200-horsepower 917/30 CanAm racing car.

Turbo Number Two, known internally as the 930/60, was a very much more refined beast than the first car to bear this name. The price of progress was felt by the customers, however: the car listed at 78,500 German Marks in 1977 had risen to 79,990 Marks a year later. In impressive command of the higher-speed range, this most powerful model in the Porsche program demonstrated one of the benefits of the turbocharged engine that had not received much attention until then: with the turbine absorbing the exhaust gas and the impeller feeding directly into the intake side of the engine, the turbocharger not only acted as a source of extra power but also as a most effective suppressor of noise. The top Porsche model is in fact much quieter and more pleasant to travel in for long distances and at high speeds than its naturally-aspirated colleagues.

Customers have valued the Turbo highly for many years now. They forgave it for only having four forward gears and by 1987 they were willing to pay 127,850 DM for a Coupé model. Some of them even rustled up a few more banknotes and ordered the Turbo Targa for 134,580 DM or – just about the ultimate

Chapter 7

– the Turbo Cabrio with soft top for 147,850 DM. It was not until 1988 that the Turbo acquired the long-awaited five-speed gearbox.

By now, Turbo prices have reached between 133,500 and 155,000 German Marks.

The first major changes to the Porsche 911 took place in the 1989 model year. The Type 964 appeared initially as the Carrera 4, with permanent four-wheel drive. The technology used to extend the driveline forward had certain similarities to the more elaborate system first seen on the Porsche 959. Transmitting power to all four wheels gives the Carrera 4 rock-solid straight-line stability. The body was optimized aerodynamically and a 250-horsepower 3.6-liter engine boosted the performance of the rejuvenated 911 almost to Turbo heights. This latter model gradually ceased production in the course of the year, not least because a version of this increasingly obsolete design capable of fulfilling all the various exhaust emission laws was impossible to realize. Development of the 360-horsepower successor model, which inherited a whole lot of technical features from the 959, was coded 965 internally and had made considerable progress before Technical Director Ulrich Bez cancelled the project because it threatened to burst through the 200,000 Mark price barrier.

1990 was therefore a dark, turbo-less year for the Porsche fan, but the gap was soon to be filled. A new Turbo appeared in 1991, with the Type 964 Carrera body, extra-wide fenders and a large rear wing. Technical progress was evident in the adoption of power steering and ABS.

74 On the last Turbo model with 3.6-liter air-cooled engine, the stylists and
75 aerodynamic experts tried to make the rear wing a little less obtrusive
and integrate it more completely into the body

This imposing 'shovel' above the tail was borne by the second version of the 3.3-liter Turbo, based on the 964 version of the Porsche 911 and built from 1990 to 1993

This Turbo had little in common with the ambitious plans of the late nineteen-eighties. Instead of the 959's ideal twin-turbocharger concept, it retained a single unit and still used the well-proven Bosch K Jetronic fuel injection system, although this had been superseded by digital engine management on all other models. This enabled the exhaust emission limits to be met, but it also meant that any increase in power could only be small. Although the 3.3-liter turbocharged engine now developed 320 horsepower, the actual gain in terms of performance on the road was not as great as in the past. The aerodynamic drag of the wider body limited the Turbo to a top speed of 270 km/h (168 mph), which was not a quantum leap forward compared with the Carrera's 260 km/h (162 mph). Demand for the car with the more corpulent body, none the less, was high. The Turbo sold well at its latest list price of 191,550 German Marks, and the Carrera 4 was therefore also made available in 'turbo look' for an extra charge of rather more than 6,000 Marks.

The return to the kind of supreme power that was available in former times took shape in 1993, when the Carrera was already about to appear as the next 993 model generation. The turbocharged engine was bored out to 100 millimeters and the stroke increased to 76.4 millimeters; once again the power output earned the accolade of 'respectable' (at 360 hp) and the torque of 520 Newton-meters was equally satis-

Chapter 7

factory. From now on the maximum speed could be quoted as 280 km/h (174 mph), and the sprint from a standstill to 100 km/h (62 mph) needed less than five seconds.

Despite revisions to the chassis, care was needed when handling the Turbo's power, since the collective force of 520 Newton-meters of torque has to be transmitted solely by the two rear tires. These, admittedly, are up to the task in terms of their size: 265/35 ZR 18.

The Porsche Turbo took the final steps toward the status of a true 'business express' during 1994, when it acquired the general technical specification of the 993 models. Electronic engine management now mobilized 408 horsepower at 5,750 rpm. Equipped with two metal-monolith catalytic converters, the flat six engine achieved the small miracle of outperforming all exhaust emission laws and being able to claim the lowest pollutant emissions among all its contemporaries.

As a belated tribute to the Porsche 959 of ten years before, the mighty torque of 540 Newton-meters was now distributed among all four wheels. This not only made it easier for the driver to control this abundant flow of power, but also made the car impressively stable on long, fast business trips along Germany's 'autobahns'. Transmitting some power to the front wheels by way of a viscous coupling fortunately did not sacrifice any of this Porsche model's true character: its drift angles revealed it to be the genuine article – a 911 that, on approaching its handling limits, called for the driver to have some experience of controlling a car in a condition of oversteer.

After twenty dynamic years, the Turbo has reached perfection and top form. At 212,000 German Marks, its price has bravely crossed the threshold that was previously considered something of a problem. In terms of power output too, the Turbo is probably some way from its final evolutionary status. For the 1995 model year the GT2 competition model with a 430-hp engine joined the program, and for a small fee of about 12,000 Marks customers were able to leave selected Porsche dealers' workshops with an extra 22 horses under the hood. A short time later customers with a good reputation as drivers of the cars with the air-cooled 'boxer' engines were able to purchase the ultimate 450-hp version of this magnificent power unit. With such power under its broad rear wing, the Porsche Turbo was capable of breaking the magic 300 kilometers-an-hour barrier (186 mph) if conditions were right. Acceleration from a standing start to 100 km/h (62 mph) also underwent a magical shift in the figures: from 5.4 to 4.5 seconds.

There may well be limits on further performance hikes in the not too distant future: exhaust emission limits scheduled to into force in the first years of the new millennium are fantastically tough. Porsche is working hard on new methods of combining performance and purity, and if history teaches us anything at all, it is that they are very likely to succeed.

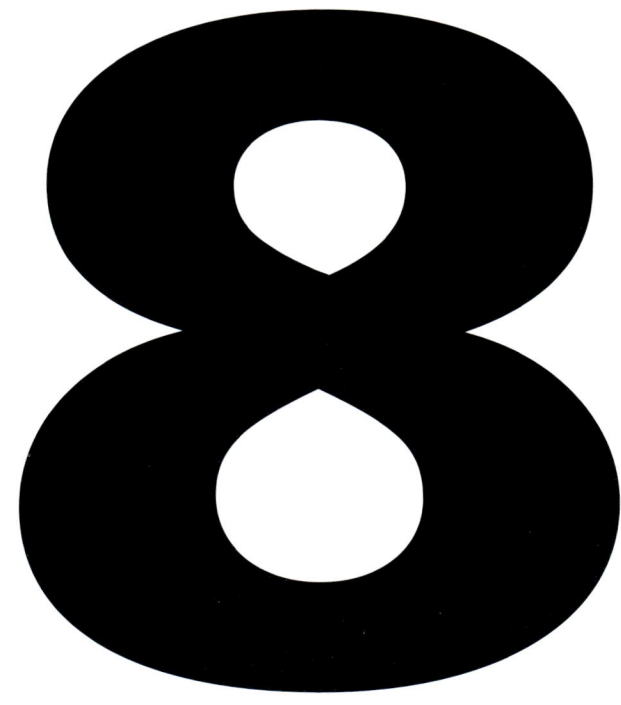

Three important chapters in a success story covering more than 20 years: the racing engines for the Carrera Turbo (1974), Porsche 956 (1982) and GT1 (1998)

With a cooling fan and a gigantic charge-air intercooler, the 1974 Carrera Turbo had a power output of 490 horsepower

Chapter 8

THE DEVELOPMENT WORK UNDERTAKEN BY the Porsche company can generally speaking be divided into two categories: some of it starts on the racetrack and ends up in production carts, the rest starts in the production-car development area – and ends up taking the checkered flag!

This is a tradition that goes back to the life's work of Professor Ferdinand Porsche, whose designs have had a major influence on motor sport in the 20th century – at Austro-Daimler, Mercedes or the Auto Union, and later on his own factory premises. "Motor sport" declares Porsche's chief executive officer Wendelin Wiedeking with the same enthusiasm today, "is to Porsche what the water is to the sea."

Turbocharging as a design principle first appeared on the Porsche 917, the twelve-cylinder racing car that owes its origins to the work of Professor Porsche's grandson, Dr. Ferdinand Piëch. From 1972 on, two turbochargers from the KKK company fed combustion air to the 917's monumental engine. What started with a swept volume of 4.5 liters and an output of 850 horsepower culminated in 1973 with 5.4 liters and 1,100 horsepower. This was enough to make competitors in the US CanAm race series look rather weak-kneed. What happened then was a typical response on the part of the motor sport authorities: they changed the rules so that the Porsche racing department's roaring monsters were cut down to size and the turbocharger had, for the moment, to abandon its victorious progress.

In 1974 the 911 appeared with a widened body, a 'whale tail' wing of enormous size and the first road-going Porsche turbocharged engine; the internal designation was the Type 930. As one might expect, competition drivers lost no time is assessing its suitability for the racetrack. Porsche too saw the new car as a promising contender for the constructors' world championship, which from 1976 on was due to be run

POWER FROM THE AIR FOR LE MANS

By Malte Jürgens

How the turbocharged six-cylinder engine became a regular winner of the most famous of all 24-hour races

according to Group 5 regulations. This meant a chance to win the Le Mans 24-hour race with a competition car derived from a standard product rather than a more exotic prototype.

The situation looked good: In 1973 two standard Carrera RSR cars without turbocharging had been able to win two world championship races, the Daytona 24-hour event and the no less eminent Targa Florio in Sicily. Faster but less reliable rivals had to retire, and in any case the new Turbo was certain to be faster than its normally-aspirated predecessors.

The first modification designed to make the new racing car out of the 930 was, surprisingly enough, to make the engine smaller. Porsche wanted to enter the sport prototype class, where an engine size limit of three liters applied, but since all forms of forced aspiration, including the turbocharger, incurred a handicap factor of 1.4, the Turbo's engine had to be reduced to 2,142 cc in size.

A suitable crankshaft was found in the earlier 2-liter production engine's parts bin, with a stroke of 66 millimeters. The engineering team was surprised by its reliability, despite having to transmit 500 horsepower, about three times the original rated value. Titanium conrods were used between the crankshaft and the Mahle company's light-alloy pistons. The aluminum cylinders had a bore of 83 millimeters and their walls were given the well-proven Nikasil coating. As on all its competition engines, Porsche gave the Turbo a simple but effective dry sumpt lube system. For long-distance races lasting up to six hours, an ultra-light magnesium engine block derived from the production design was used, but for the Le Mans 24-hour race Porsche reverted to an injection-molded aluminum block.

The cylinder heads, air cooled and bolted to the block like the cylinders, had two valves per cylinder and came from the familiar 2.34- and 2.5-liter competition engines. They bore a strong resemblance to standard production components, except for the twin-spark ignition and the larger-diameter sodium-cooled valves, made from titanium on the inlet side and Nimonic on the exhaust side. Valve clearances were adjusted by means of small caps of differing thickness, to vary the distance between the cams on the four-bearing camshafts and the bucket-type tappets. High-tension capacitor-type ignition, first tried out on the RSR in 1973, supplied ignition current to a total of twelve spark plugs per engine.

The turbocharged racing engine passed through its development phase in double-quick time, since many elements of the turbocharging system were adopted from the 917/10 engine. The 'biturbo' had twice the displacement of the Carrera Turbo, but this simply meant using one half of the twelve-cylinder system for the new six-cylinder engine. The KKK turbocharger was set to deliver a boost pressure of between 1.3 and 1.4 bar. A Garrett coil spring and diaphragm bypass valve limited boost pressure when the critical threshold was reached, and diverted part of the exhaust gas used to drive the turbine directly to atmosphere.

From a central pressure chamber, six intake pipes each with its own throttle butterfly led to the engine's cylinders. When the throttles were closed, a flap valve opened automatically to dissipate the remaining pressure. This avoided pressure peaks when closing the throttle and increased the reliable operating life of the turbine rotor, one of the turbocharger's most sensitive components.

Increasing power output means generating more heat which has to be disposed of by special measures. Inside the engine, a larger volume of oil was therefore forced through the lubricating circuit by a high-performance oil pump taken from Porsche's 908 eight-cylinder racing engine.

The charge air from the turbocharger was at a temperature as high as 150 degrees Centigrade, and therefore had to be brought back down to the region of 50 degrees by a giant air-to-air heat exchanger. This principle was not only adopted to keep the Carrera engine cool but also to enhance its efficiency: cooler combustion air has a higher density, contains more oxygen and therefore devlops more power.

A basic compression ratio of 6.5:1, cam profiles slightly less steep than on the non-turbocharged RSR racing engines and control of the Bosch six-plunger fuel injection pump according to boost pressure were also features of this new Turbo package. Test-rig trials of the 911 ATL engine (the initials standing for the German term for turbocharger) yielded an output of 490 horsepower by 1974, achieved at a relatively moderate engine speed of 7,600 rpm. Peak torque was in the region of 470 Newton-meters at 5,400 rpm. The clutch retained its standard diameter of 225 mm (8.86 in) but had uprated springs and a sintered metal facing; it transmitted all this power without complaint. It was the gearbox, on the other hand, that prevented the Carrera Turbo from winning Le Mans in 1974. Fifth gear was lost, after which the racing 911 was overtaken by the French Matra V12 and could only manage second place, just as it had in the Watkins Glen six-hour race.

Porsche continued development work on the turbocharged flat-six racing engine and soon transformed it into a regular race-winner. In 1976 the Type 936 won the sports car world championships and the 935 the constructors' world championships, and also triumphed in Le Mans with Jacky Ickx and Gijs van Lennep at the wheel; a 936 was victorious again in Le Mans a year later. In 1977, 1978 und 1979 the constructors' world champion was the Porsche 935, and even as late as 1981 the 'elderly' 936 won the world's most celebrated long-distance race once again.

For 1982 there was a new Group C prototype ruling that laid down a fuel consumption limit for each race. The engines were not allow to guzzle more than 51 liters per 100 kilometers (about 4.6 US miles per gallon). Ten years before, the Porsche 917 had needed more than 90 liters for the same distance (2.6 mpg).

Porsche's response was to develop a prototype with a design number that has become legend: the 956.

This two-seater sports car's engine was based on the successful Type 936 that had so often and so spectacularly demonstrated its reliability in long-distance races in particular. The 956's racing engine had little

Water-cooled cylinder heads with four valves per cylinder made the 620-horsepower turbocharged engine for the 956 into the legendary winner of one event after another from 1982 on

Full water cooling, an output of 600 hp in competition trim and 544 hp in the road car – this was the GT1 Turbo for the 1998 model year

Chapter 8

more than the number of cylinders in common with the Carrera Turbo: six, as one might have expected.

The new rules allowed the engine's displacement to grow to 2.65 liters. The original 66 mm stroke was retained but the bore was increased to 92.3 millimeters. The cylinder heads now had four valves per cylinder and were no longer air-cooled. As on the 936 engine, they had acquired a water jacket to keep peak temperatures at bay. The cylinder barrels, however, although welded to the heads, were still air-cooled by a fan.

With a basic compression ratio of 7.2:1 and two KKK turbochargers to supply boost at up to 1.2 bar, the engine delivered a healthy 620 hp at 8,200 rpm; its maximum speed lay 200 rpm higher, and at about 8,500 rpm a governor put a stop to all attempts to rev the engine to even higher speeds.

The engine was built along the lines that had so often proved successful for Porsche's competition units: a vertically split, pressure-cast crankcase and a forged steel crankshaft running in seven main bearings.

Foreged pistons and titanium conrods were essential for an engine designed to stay ahead at Le Mans speeds for twenty-four hours. The four overhead camshafts were driven by a gear train to ensure maximum precision. Almost buried beneath two radiators, two oil coolers and two charge-air intercoolers, this racing engine was a magnificent performer right from the start. The factory cars with the chassis numbers 956.002, 956.003 and 956.004 took the first three places in Le Mans on their first outing there in 1982. Team manager Peter Falk, who occupied this post for many years, declares this successful summer's day and night on the Sarthe circuit to be "the finest day in my career!"

The engine used in the Porsche 956 and its successor, the 962, maintained this winning streak for almost ten years, won a world championship event in Dijon, France, as late as 1989.

To convince ourselves of the truly 'never-ending' nature of the turbocharged-engine saga from Porsche's competition department in Weissach, however, we must look at the amazing performance put up by the GT1. In 1997 Porsche decided that it was time to win Le Mans once again; this was a year in which the rules called for at least one sports car to have been registered legally for the road before being used as a basis for the race entry. The outcome was a series of exotic *one-shots*: Nissan, for instance, built the R 390, Mercedes the CLK-GTR, and Porsche set to work and developed the GT1.

Its chassis was a hybrid of the 911's sheet steel bodyshell and a rigid tubular frame. For the engine, Porsche once again decided that a well-proven principle should be updated. The GT1 engine's bore and stroke, 95 x 74.4 millimeters for a displacement of 3,163 cc, had already proved highly successful in the Type 962.

In contrast to the earlier 956, the cylinders too were now fully water-cooled, using a crossflow principle from the hotter to the cooler side; Porsche had adopted the same principle for the 962 before the Group C rules were changed. The vertically split crankcase now had three cylinder barrels at left and right with Nikasil-coated cylinder liners; to these were bolted the four-valve DOHC cylinder heads, which were also water-cooled. The road version of this engine developed 544 horsepower at 7,000 rpm, the racing version is alleged to have reached almost 600 hp at 7,200 rpm. Maximum torque of 600 Nm at 4,250 rpm was impressive enough on the roadgoing version, but the racing engine surpassed this with 650 Nm at 5,500 rpm.

The performance data of the only slightly tamed road car were quite outstanding: Porsche quoted the time for accelerating the GT1 from 0 to 100 km/h (0 – 62 mph) as 3.7 seconds, and its top speed as 310 km/h (196 mph). With a different transmission ratio, the racing version was good for up to 340 km/h (211 mph). Engine management was entrusted to the Motronic 5.2 system, the intake air mass measured by a continuous-acting hot film device and the sequential multi-point fuel injection had oxygen-sensing control by lambda probe to ensure that the metal-monolith catalysts performed efficiently.

Each combustion chamber was now content with a single spark plug, there was electronic idle-speed stabilizing and cylinder-selective knock control to vary the ignition and injection timing and avoid engine damage if lower-octane fuel had to be used. The dry sump lube system held 15 liters (15.7 US quarts) of oil, and electric ring-gear pumps delivered the GT1 engine's fuel to the intake ports.

Oh yes, Le Mans 1998 – we almost forgot. After 24 hours at top racing speeds, the first two cars across the line were – the Porsche GT1's! Other competitors' cars were faster but not as reliable. There were also other reliable cars – but they weren't as fast!

´Top´ is the name for the new Turbo in Weissach. It's certainly full of ´top ideas´

THE 'TOP' MANAGERS
By Clauspeter Becker

HORST MARCHART
Member of the Executive Board for Research and Development

Chapter 9

THE PEOPLE IN WEISSACH CALL THEIR LATEST TURBO AFFECTIONATELY 'TOP'. This time it isn't one of those cryptic abbreviations that technical departments love so much, but the perfect expression of the team's target: to celebrate the year 2000 by launching the most powerful, fastest and most perfect production model in Porsche's history.

Horst Marchart, whose renewal of the Porsche model program has made him one of the architects of the company's success, planned the steps up onto the victor's podium back in the early nineteen-nineties: the Boxster in 1996, the Carrera in 1997 and the Turbo in 2000.

On this determined path to perfection, the technical experts allowed their top model a reasonable period of time to ripen and mature. The final catalog of requirements was drawn up early in 1997, when the Carrera was not far from the start of series production. The engineers and marketing strategists did not take long to reach agreement: as well as traditional sporting qualities, the new car was to represent

Horst Marchart was born in Austria and is 61 years of age.
He joined Porsche as a young engineer back in 1969 and became
Director of the Weissach Development Center in 1988.

the state of the art in automobile development in the road-safety and journey-quality areas as well. Horst Marchart and his colleagues knew then that the new model, like its predecessor, would have four-wheel drive. They also knew that a Turbo for the new millennium would need design features that would have been rejected out of hand as heresy by supersport aficionados 25 years ago. Now, fortunately, such items as traction control, dynamic stability management and even automatic transmission are regarded as desirable even in the elite group of those who buy and drive the world's fastest sports cars.

With more determination than ever before, the stylists and aerodynamics experts worked on giving the new Porsche Turbo a restrained, dignified appearance. Even the top models previous trade mark, the large rear wing, was a victim of this new understatement, though it is typical of Weissach's thinking that the replacement is a high-tech double-blade wing with an extending element.

When it came to power output and top speed, Horst Marchart courageously laid down sensible limits. The new Turbo engine clearly had to have slightly more horses or kilowatts on call than the previous model, but in the form of logical growth, not escalation. The development emphasis was on torque rather than ultimate power. The peak output of 309 kW (420 hp) has a solid foundation: a torque curve in the form of an extended plateau at approximately 550 Newton-meters, all the way from 2,800 to 5,000 revolutions per minute. As for top speed, 300 kilometers an hour (186 mph) were still a reasonable target. "304 km/h is a good figure," says Marchart. "301 would have been just as good!"

A very fundamental decision when planning a new Porsche Turbo was of course which engine should serve as the basis. The new water-cooled flat-six unit was the obvious choice, but there was also the racing engine that already had 16 Le Mans victories to its credit.

"We could have extracted the same peak performance from the standard production engine," Marchart explains, "but there were good reasons for choosing the racing engine even though it is more expensive. Its displacement is easier to vary for competition purposes, and when high rates of lateral acceleration are encountered on the racing circuit, its dry sump lubrication with a separate oil tank keeps engine oil pressure more stable on corners."

Horst Marchart and his engineers in Weissach have given all Turbo drivers special reason to be proud of their cars: the engine's design is based on innumerable motor-sport successes.

Chapter 9

FRIEDRICH BEZNER

General Project Manager, Porsche 911 Turbo

"THE SIMULTANEOUS ENGINEERING PRINCIPLE has certainly made a tremendous difference to our methods of work", declares Friedrich Bezner, who has overall responsibility for the Porsche 911 Turbo project. "Right from the start all our departments work together, and the cost picture has to be finalized before design work starts." In the project office, where this advance work is carried out, the costs for the Turbo went three complete rounds before the agreement was reached and the final bell sounded. Then came the project scheduling phase, and the development objectives were laid down.

"We can shorten the times we need considerably now, because design work on the computer speeds up every stage of the process." Bezner formulates the targets that Porsche has set itself for the millennium as follows: "With the new Turbo engine we weren't looking primarily for higher power. We wanted to build a refined engine with more torque at the driver's disposal and we definitely wanted to lower the fuel consumption still further, to provide an adequate action radius from a smaller fuel tank." 'At least ten percent more economical' was the challenge the engine developers had to face. Porsche's technicians tackled the task — and cut fuel consumption by twelve percent!

Pinky Lai is 49 and has been working for Porsche since 1989 in the Weissach Design Studio run by Harm Lagaay. He has played a major part in determining the appearance of the current Porsche 911 models.

Friedrich Bezner is 59, and joined Porsche as an apprentice in 1954; he took his engineering degree later, and after this managed many projects including the Porsche 959

PINKY LAI

Project Manager, Styling

"Until now, the Porsche Turbo looked like an athlete, a sprinter in running gear. The new Turbo is different: it's still an athlete, certainly, and covers the hundred meters in record time, but it does so in a business suit!" Designer Pinky Lai came over 28 years ago from far-off Hong Kong, which has now reverted to China, and his place of work is Porsche's development center in Weissach. In his view a supersport model capable of exceeding 300 kilometers an hour easily should preserve a fairly dignified character and certainly have nothing 'macho' about it. "Those days are gone, and such over displays of strength are something the customer who can afford to buy a Turbo wouldn't approve of." Lai is convinced that "if we want to emphasize the Turbo's personality, we can do it with more restrained visual features like the charge air intake on the side of the body and the new elevating spoiler on the tail, which are all technically essential anyway."

Chapter 9

GERD SEIFERT

Project Manager, Suspension

Gerd Seifert 47 years of age, joined Porsche in 1990. When choosing the ideal settings for the Turbo's suspension he aims for the best possible synthesis of sporting, safe ride and comfort on long journeys. With success, as we can now see

Walter Kirchner (52) has been with Porsche since 1971. When the new Porsche Turbo was under development, he was the transmission expert faced with the task of matching a five-speed automatic transmission to the needs of a supersport model

WALTER KIRCHNER

Project Manager, Transmission

PLENTY OF PROBLEMS AROSE for colleague Johannes Paul as a result of Gerd Seifert's determined onslaughts on the world braking record, if there is such a thing, in Nardo. "25 heavy brake applications in a row don't only call for massive brakes but for large amounts of cooling air as well", he says. But problems are made to be mastered, and in teamwork with body developer Nennemann and aerodynamicist Preiss, the still-young Turbo was persuaded to 'keep cool'. Plenty of air now reaches all the brake disks – though Seifert was first obliged to design a wheel hub carrier with improved airflow.

"560 NEWTON-METERS OF TORQUE are a challenge for the Turbo with Tiptronic S transmission," says Walter Kirchner, "but the mechanical load didn't worry us as much as the cooling. We solved this problem with a suitably large heat exchanger." The result is the Turbo Tiptronic S, surely one of the most mature, elegant engineering solutions that even Porsche has so far produced.

HARRY NENNEMANN

Project Manager, Body Construction

"It could have been worse!" says Harry Nennemann, obviously satisfied. The development task that faced him was to keep the new Turbo's drag coefficient down to $c_D = 0.33$. The results came out so well that Harry Nennemann and aerodynamics expert Michael Preiss would surely have been highly praised by the wind tunnel if it could speak.

The measurements confirmed what may have gone under in the rushing, mighty wind inside the tunnel: the drag coefficient is only 0.31! A sensational result, only slightly below that for the Carrera despite the Turbo's larger radiators and charge-air intercooler – and with even lower axle lift values thrown in.

Peter Zickwolf is 49 years of age and has been with Porsche since he graduated in 1976.
He expects the new adjustable valve lift system to appear in other engines soon

PETER ZICKWOLF

Project Manager, Engine

"Adjustable valve lift was difficult to master at first, because there wasn't sufficient oil pressure to make the adjustment work below engine speeds of about 2,000 rpm," Peter Zickwolf recalls. "The torque used to leap up by as much as 160 Newton-meters." To prevent the heads of Turbo drivers being flung back like astronauts exposed to the many times the usual gravitational force, the oil pressure had to be modified and the changeover initiated at a lower engine speed – 1,200 rpm. There too the increase in torque is 60 Nm, but it can be smoothed out so successfully by the electronics that the driver isn't aware of it. In this way, Peter Zickwolf has achieved another of his ambitious objectives: "Our aim has always been for the engine to deliver its power in a civilized manner."

Chapter 9

SIEGFRIED STECKDAUB

Project Manager, Electrics and Electronics

SIEGFRIED STECKDAUB is the guy who killed off the dipstick! There is no risk of the Turbo owner getting dirty hands when checking the engine's oil level. It is now measured by sensors in the tank, and displayed as a brief video game on the car's computer monitor. And just in case even this graphic warning is ignored, a bright red light comes on too if the oil in the engine's lube system drops below an acceptable minimum level.

Cars are becoming highly networked objects, and their electronics have to handle increasing quantities of information. Steckdaub has arranged, for instance, for the computer to check the lateral acceleration sensors before monitoring the oil level, so that the reading is not falsified by the Turbo being hustled through a series of sharp bends at that moment.

The driver pushes the gas pedal down innocently, so to speak, and its electronics and the Motronic management consult briefly on the best moment for the valve lift to be varied. The unavoidable power surge is compensated for by intelligent modulation of the throttle opening angle — the electronics again!

Siegfried Steckdaub (39) has been with Porsche since 1984. His namesake in German mythology wrestled with the fabled 'lindworm', and his career is largely devoted to contending with the complexities of the modern car's wiring harness — often an equally daunting task!

10

In the wind tunnel, aerodynamics are no longer the only research topics

OUR EARTH'S ATMOSPHERE sometimes seems rather thin, but it none the less offers considerable resistance to all forms of fast-moving transport. If the humble family car is propelled at the relatively modest speed of 100 kilometers an hour (62 miles an hour), it needs between 75 and 80 percent of its power simply to overcome resistance to movement through the air. At 300 km/h (186 mph) this struggle to penetrate the air, the resistance of which increases with the square of the speed, needs more than 90 percent of the engine's power, whereas rolling resistance – the contact between the tires and the road – only goes up linearly with increasing speed.

These are immutable laws of physics, and therefore the logic of reducing the aerodynamic drag of extremely fast cars is self-evident. They need the smallest possible frontal area and a particularly good streamlined form, so that the drag coefficient (the 'c_D' value) can be kept low.

In reality, things are not quite as clear-cut as that. Although sports cars are usually low-built and therefore present a smaller frontal area to the wind, the aerodynamics of the body, which determine the drag coefficient are not always as good as on slower, less sporting cars. A Porsche Carrera has a c_D of 0.30, the latest Turbo of 0.31. Yet compact, not particularly powerful coupé models achieve values as low as 0.25, and so do quite large sedans. There seems to be a contradiction here, but it is explained by recourse to the same laws of physics as before: very fast, powerful sports cars are unable to make full use of the designer's talents in reducing aerodynamic drag for a variety of good reasons. The technical specifications that cause Porsche's experts to work long hours in the wind tunnel contain far more requirements that have to be satisfied than the relative-

SNATCHED FROM THE AIR

How aerodynamic research makes it possible to drive safely at 300 kilometers an hour

By Clauspeter Becker

ly straightforward demand for low drag resistance. The relationship between aerodynamics and road safety is the first important consideration. The design engineer knows that a conflict of objectives is likely to arise here at a very early stage, since the traditional shape of a passenger car is more of an obstacle than an asset. Seen from the side, the automobile has a most undesirable similarity with the wing of an aircraft, with a larger surface area on top than underneath in both cases. In other words, the air is bound to flow across the upper surface at a higher speed. This effect is what generates lift and, in the case of the airplane, is most welcome, whereas for an automobile it threatens to worsen tire grip, dynamic stability – and safety.

For optimum safety the very opposite tendency would be better, but an automobile has to pay a high price for strong aerodynamic downforce. A Formula 1 racing car has it, but it is of little practical value for a conventional car. A sports car such as the GT1 has it to some extent too, but this model too would be somewhat out of place in heavy commuter traffic. Furthermore, strong downforce in fact increases drag, fuel consumption and therefore emissions increase and the car's top speed is lower. Michael Preiss, who heads Porsche's aerodynamics department in Weissach, has to use his wind tunnel in a constant search for the golden mean. His team has effectively banished aerodynamic lift at both axles of all Porsche models. His comment: "This is particularly important! A car should be tuned for good aerodynamic balance. Our latest cars achieve excellent results with a very slight bias in favor of the rear axle."

The new Porsche Turbo performs well in this respect, with only minimum front axle lift of $cA_F = 0.02$ and very slight rear-axle downforce of $cA_R = -0.01$. What this means in practice: as the car approaches its top speed of 300 km/h (168 mph), pressure on the rear axle builds up to at least nine kilograms or 90 Newton.

Preiss explains: "The advantage of the settings we have chosen is that there is an increasing understeer tendency as the speed rises, and so directional stability is improved and sudden avoidance maneuvers are safer."

Rear-axle downforce is achieved on the Turbo by relatively subtle means: a small rear spoiler on the end of the hood panel has the same effect as the extending spoiler used on the Carrera. This effect, however, is greatly enhanced by a small wing that rises out of a recess in the spoiler when 120 km/h (75 mph) are reached. This generates the 'gap effect' frequently encountered on competition cars, with a strongly accelerated upward flow of air that results in a definite increase in aerodynamic downforce.

This pressure on the tail end of the car naturally has a tendency to reduce the weight pressing down on the front wheels, so that compensating measures have to be taken. The new Turbo has them in the form of a deep front air dam with spoiler lip, the latter being made from resilient synthetic material in case it comes into contact with the road. The need for stability at high speeds makes it harder to keep aerodynamic resistance down, and the large quantities of cooling air which a powerful sports car ingests are also a factor that upsets the aerodynamic equilibrium. The air cannot pass through the radiators without incurring a certain amount of resistance. The new charge-air intercooling concept presented particular problems for Michael Preiss and his team. The call for tail-end styling without an oversize spoiler and the absence of the useful airflow through the cooling fan in the engine compartment meant that a new and altogether more complex solution was needed. Experimental work soon revealed that the air, although invited to enter openings behind the doors and flow through plastic ducts to the charge-air intercoolers behind the rear wheels, was for some

98

The two-level rear wing generates useful downforce at the rear wheels without seriously affecting overall aerodynamic resistance

100 Even if the airflow strikes the car at an angle, the lift values at the
101 axles must not increase too much or else stability in cross-winds could be a problem

unknown reason disinclined to do so. "The air inlet was in a rather unfavorable position where the flow velocity over the body is very high, so that there was little tendency for any useful amount of air to be diverted into the ducts. We considered fitting scoops, but they would have had a serious effect on the drag coefficient." Michael Preiss's report on this experimental work continues: "We therefore had rethink the problem and reposition the air outlets in a low-pressure zone, so that the cooling air was drawn in more effectively."

Such challenging aerodynamic development work seldom proceeds without minor problems cropping up. This was the case with the front spoiler lips, Preiss recalls. The design was about to be finalized when his colleagues responsible for brake systems development discovered that the brake disks were being starved of cooling air. Although cutting two inlets in the plastic spoiler and fitting suitable air ducts to them provided the brakes with a lot more air, the aerodynamic effect of the spoiler lip was much worse than before. This dilemma was solved by fitting a narrow strip pointing forward horizontally. The road test teams praised this too: "The spoiler is much more scratch-resistant than it was before!"

Is aerodynamic work now nothing but painstaking detail or are major breakthroughs still possible? Michael Preiss knows the answer: "The outside mirrors annoy us most! They increase the frontal area and ruin the drag coefficient. A video system would be possible technically, and no financial problem for Porsche. But virtual reality on a monitor simply doesn't match the spatial quality of a simple mirror image ..."

Flat out at 300 km/h, the bluish-white beams of the xenon headlamps feel their way forward

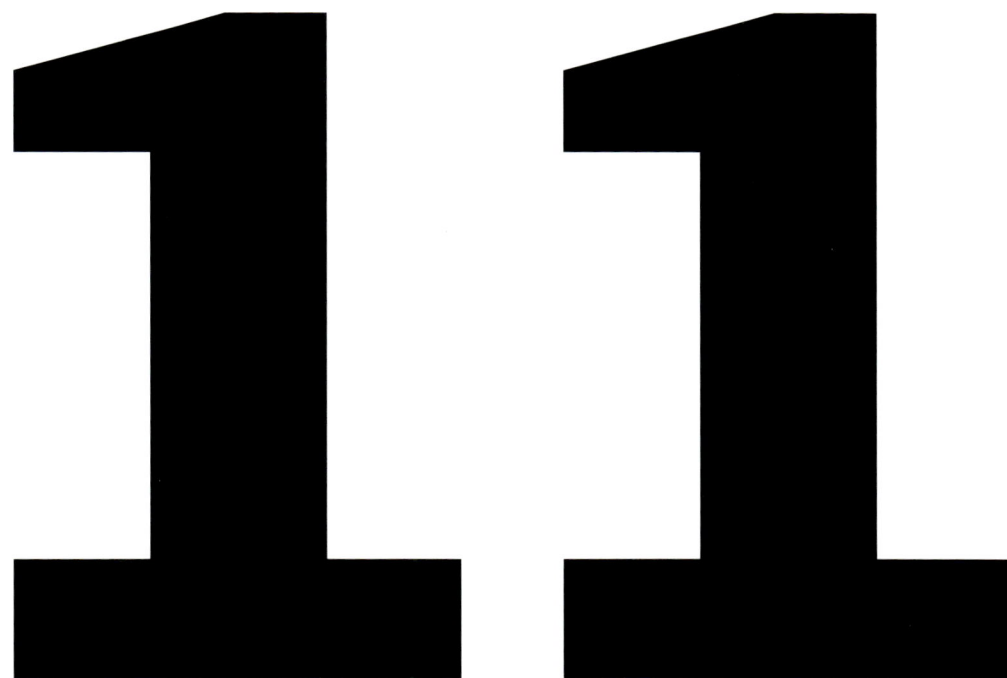

Chapter 11

EXPERIMENTAL ENGINEER JOHANNES PAUL LIKES HIS PLACE OF WORK TO HAVE A TOUCH OF CLASS. In the winter of 1999/2000, two such places were at his disposal. Seated on superb leather upholstery, wearing a crash helmet and a flameproof overall, he took the new Porsche Turbo through its final maturity tests at high speed and checked its thermodynamic efficiency.

There were two Turbos for him to drive alternately: a sporting one with six-speed manual gearbox and a noble one with five-speed automatic transmission. They contain a quantity of equipment of a kind that even Porsche's Tequipment, Exclusive or Selection catalogs don't offer.

The Measuring Technology department at Porsche's Development Center in Weissach has been at this car: it now boasts computers and measuring sensors worth several hundred thousand German Marks, and has sacrificed its entire front trunk and most of the space behind the driver's and front passenger's seats. Lengthy cables wind their way through the interior, and the sense of style imparted by the leather upholstery has definitely suffered slightly.

The usual instruments have been joined by a large monitor screen, and there is a computer keyboard too, though Johannes Paul doesn't have to operate it while driving the car. His task is quite clear: full speed round the 12.6 km (7.8 mile) circuit at the Prototipo proving ground in Nardo, which is located well down on Italy's 'boot heel'.

Speeds of 300 km/h (186 mph) close to the crash barriers call for a certain degree of concentration, but there is no other traffic, since the high-speed track has been booked exclusively for the day. On 'mixed traffic' days, when various makes of car share the track in a friendly fashion, a speed limit of a paltry 240 km/h (150 mph) is imposed.

3,000 KM A DAY

Top speed as an everyday event. A report from Nardo, Southern Italy, on Porsche's high-speed test runs

By Clauspeter Becker

A Turbo naturally needs more than this to stretch its legs. Nardo can therefore only accommodate Porsche's engineering teams when the rest of the world has stopped work, for example on a Saturday night and early Sunday morning. Flat out at 300 km/h (nearly 170 mph), the bluish-white beams of the xenon headlamps feel their way forward. Just below the upper crash barrier of the banked circuit, there are no markings to provide an indication of the car's speed. No one is there either to overtake or, more important still, to be overtaken. Top speed – not much more than a routine task.

Of course, there can never be any question of relaxing completely when driving alone on this closed-off circuit. Although its curves are banked and therefore in theory permit the car to be driven hands-off at 200 km/h (124 mph), increasing the speed to 300 km/h (186 mph) is quite a different matter and needs a firm hand on the steering wheel. Driving 'along the wall', aided by the centrifugal force that presses the car down onto the track's surface, in fact causes no problems of directional stability.

What irritates Johannes Paul most is that this centrifugal force compresses the car's springs and reduces suspension travel: "On rough patches the whole car shakes and the instruments are blurred!"

Chapter 11

The Turbo with manual-shift gearbox puts up the fastest average lap times. The official printout from the proving ground management puts the figure even higher than the car's technical specification would suggest: 310 km/h (192.6 mph). But even at the wheel of the automatic-transmission car, Paul succeeds in breaking the 300 kilometer-an-hour barrier. He likes the Tiptronic Turbo a lot: "Its power comes on in an unbelievably commanding way, but the automatic box handles it just perfectly."

Paul's journeys around the banked high-speed track never last more than about half an hour. When he has covered about 150 kilometers (just over 90 miles) and is on his twelfth lap, it's high time to refuel in order to avoid the embarrassment of coasting to a halt with the tank run dry. At top speed on the uppermost lane of the track, fuel consumption is not quite at the impressive levels normally recorded in the standard European tests.

The measuring equipment confirms that everything has operated correctly. The engineers from the thermodynamics department, Manfred Hochkönig, Christian Thies and Jürgen Schwirtz, are happy: despite the high average speed the coolant, engine oil and charge air temperatures are very little different from the typical values recorded in road traffic. Only the from the gearbox and the front differential temperature readings are slightly higher than the road-test values at the end of the run.

This doesn't worry Manfred Hochkönig: "We're still a long way below the critical limits. In any case, it's very unlikely that anyone else in the world is about to drive our car flat out at 310 kilometers an hour

104 The Nardo circuit is completely circular, with a diameter of 4.0 km (2.5 miles) and a length of 12.6 km (7.83 miles)

106 The true high-speed laps are driven in the evening and
107 continue late into the night

The test cars are packed with computers and masses of wiring occupying every corner

for 150 kilometers! If they do, we'd like to know some more about the kind of road they do it on!" While Johannes Paul is lapping the track on his lonely vigil, Karl Haun has an arduous task ahead of him: the brake test. Porsche's version of this is unique, and calls for a high level of endurance both from the brakes themselves and from the person who applies them during the test.

At 90 percent of the car's top speed, that is to say in the case of the new Porsche Turbo at 277 km/h (172 mph), the car is slowed with the brakes to 100 km/h (62 mph). Without any pause for breath the speed is then increased again to the original value, which takes an average of only 32 seconds in the Turbo, and the brake application repeated. When they are given such severe treatment, the brake disks remain red-hot all the time. Be that as it may, they have to put up with this extreme form of stop-and-go treatment twenty-five times in a row.

The torture suffered by the entire brake system is efficiently recorded while the car is on the move by the on-board computer: disk and brake fluid temperatures, brake fluid and pedal pressures.

When driver Karl Haun brings the car to a standstill after 25 of these sadistic test cycles, one would scarcely believe that he had been closely involved in this attempt to expose the slightest weakness. Test technician Wolfgang Grawe downloads data from the computer's memory and feeds the results on to the

screen for brake test engineer Gerhard Schäfer to examine more closely. "Something wrong at the front left!" is the conclusion, diagnosed by Grawe laconically as "Number Four doesn't answer."

One of the five thermocouples in the brake disk has given up the ghost; these devices have to withstand temperatures of up to 600 to 750 degrees Centigrade and convert them into electrical signals for the on-board computer. But four very satisfactory readings from the remaining sensors cause Grawe to exclaim: "It's always good when the brakes are more reliable than the test gear!"

While the evaluation process continues, mechanics Bernd Weimar and Luigi Franzini carry out the maintenance routine in double-quick time: wheels off, brake pads renewed, disks measured, wheels back on. After 25 almost full brake applications, the pads have lost about a millimeter of their original thickness; otherwise they are in very good condition. Disk thickness is within the specified tolerance.

The failed number-four thermocouple is sent out for another spin, the team's attitude being that the remaining ones will supply all the necessary data. Disk renewal is not due until the next routine pit-stop. After this, the pace will hot up even more, with full brake applications that cause the ABS to cut in. Sensor number four in the right brake disk has also stopped sending signals. Six of these extra-severe brake-test cycles with 25 full brake applications are scheduled for this particular night driving session; afterwards, on the way back to the hotel, Karl Haun begs his colleague Wolfgang Grawe to "go easy on the brakes" of their VW Sharan!

A typical Turbo speed: 300 km/h

110 *A flashing light on the roof is obligatory in Nardo, and the ventilated brake disks glow at almost white*
111 *heat as the test routine proceeds*

The legendary Nardo test track

Its official name is now "Prototipo", and it was originally built by Fiat but now belongs to an international investment company. In the Italian province of Apulia, it is 35 kilometers (22 miles) to the north-west of the town of the same name and about the same distance west of Lecce, famous for its baroque architecture.

Like all such facilities of this kind "Prototipo" in fact consists of several tracks and circuits. The high-speed circuit is circular, 4,000 meters (13,125 feet) in diameter and 12,600 meters (41,340 feet) long. It forms the outer perimeter and encloses another small circuit for trucks, dynamic test runs and an off-road track. Plans have been drawn up to extend the facility.

Almost every European motor-vehicle manufacturer hires "Prototipo", which also offers them large workshop buildings. The long journey to the south of Italy is no disadvantage, since the climate is so mild that work can normally continue throughout the winter.

The Nardo proving ground is not fully fenced off to prevent outsiders from gaining access to it, and therefore attracts 'prototype hunters'; many have taken up permanent quarters in the surrounding region.

12

For the new Turbo the PSM is quite
clearly a state-of-the-art feature in the year 2000

TRUST IN THE GOOD WORKS performed by modern electronics took some time to gain ground at Porsche. When the Porsche 959 was designed, it incorporated just about everything that could reasonably be described as technological progress, but even then the boundaries between the driver's skill and the electronic support provided by the car were drawn along fairly traditional lines. Anti-lock braking was included, since it was already a well-proven device. Traction control, on the other hand, which had just been developed and made to work, was not allowed to interfere between the turbocharged engine's 300 Newton-meters of torque and the four driven wheels "... because it just isn't suitable for a sports car!"

There are still a few sports-car manufacturers who take such a conservative view. Porsche, however, caught up with the future long ago, and takes the attitude: "Since a Porsche is a sports car that must be suitable for normal day-to-day driving, it should have every device that contributes to safety." Whether or not traction control should be provided therefore becomes a superfluous question. Even cars with far less power than the 959 now have it as a matter of course.

The next step forward in providing the driver with the appropriate level of electronic assistance took place in 1998, when the Carrera 4 was offered with the "Porsche Stability Management" dynamic control system, which provides the driver with a considerably higher degree of electronic assistance in critical situations.

For the new Turbo PSM is quite clearly a state-of-the-art feature in the year 2000. Of course, the magnificent chassis and suspension of a Porsche and the immense reserves of safety it offers make any

LET THE PROCESSOR PLAY PROFESSOR

How Porsche Stability Management makes fast driving safer

By Clauspeter Becker

such dynamic stability system the final element in a perfect combination rather than just a kind of electronic life-raft with which to save oneself from a sinking ship.

Controlling the dynamic movements of a fast car is a difficult process, not to be taken lightly; the task of any such electronic system can be defined as intervening automatically to avoid a potentially hazardous driving situation. When designing such systems and determining their settings, it's important to define the risk that one wishes to avoid. A sensible approach is to make the car as foolproof as possible, if this seems to be necessary. The automatic brake applications that stabilize the car then take place well before it reaches its handling limits. Although this offers the relatively inexperienced driver a high level of security, it is unfortunately not in accordance with the policy of 'driving in its finest form' that one associates with Porsche and its products.

The engineers were committed to upholding the traditional standards of cars from Zuffenhausen, which lay down that a Porsche is easy to control but none the less calls for a modicum of driving talent. Such factors as tire width also have a part to play – and so Porsche's technical people decided that the car should be permitted to reach the handling limit before the possible sins of the driver underwent any compulsory corrective action. Against total stupidity, alas, even PSM is powerless.

The cars of those who enter a bend at 120 kilometers an hour instead of the more appropriate 80 are more likely to need Porsche's repair service than its stability management program.

The PSM switch on the dashboard is there for drivers to use if they are confident of what they do at the wheel. To turn off this switch is to declare "This is a quitclaim deed on all electronic lifesavers." It would perhaps be too strong a term to call this a brave decision, but it does give the driver access to a Turbo that will drift quite dramatically on corners if enough power is used to slide the rear wheels sideways – and the power is undeniably there! However, rescue is in sight: Porsche's programmers have had pity on those who get into a hopeless situation with PSM switched off and can feel the car getting out of control. As soon as the brake pedal is pressed down, PSM springs to life again and stability management takes over in an attempt to get the car back on to the straight and narrow path.

Whether the keen driver who dispenses with PSM can actually hustle the Turbo along faster is doubtful, especially in typical modern traffic. This is because the car's neutral handling limits are so high that no responsible driver would normally reach them on the public highway.

When the road is wet, however, even the skilled driver finds it difficult to coax the car along as quickly and safely with throttle, brake and steering wheel alone; PSM can make the task easier. Ice and snow

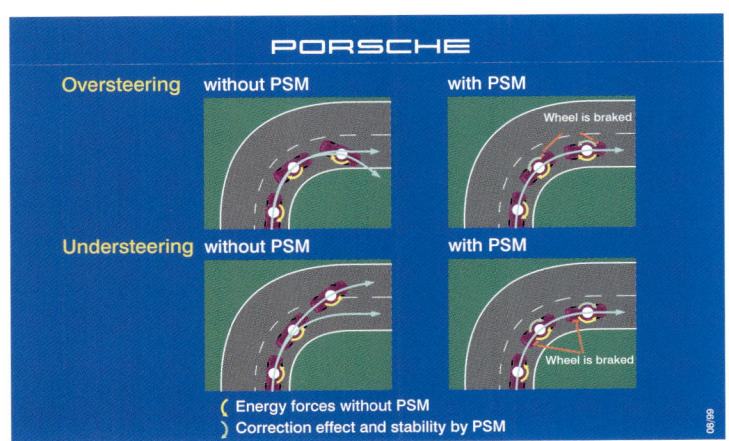

Porsche Stability Management keeps the car's self-steering effects neutral when cornering or if an emergency avoidance maneuver is needed on either a high- or low-grip surface. It counteracts oversteer by controlled braking of the outer front wheel, and understeer by giving the same treatment to the inside rear wheel

on the road can demand the utmost driving skill even from such rally stars as Walter Röhrl, who are quite prepared to admit that the remarkable Porsche Stability Management then wins the day.

Agreed, driving the Porsche Turbo without using PSM can be a true pleasure, particularly on a dry road with plenty of tire grip, but such roads should either be devoid of any other traffic, or else the driver should hire a few laps of a private racing circuit to sample the car's handling delights. Without PSM, for example, Walter Röhrl can lap the North Loop of the Nürburg Ring in eight minutes. And those who attend a driver training course to qualify for a genuine 'Turbo pilot's license' will naturally emulate the former world rally champion and revel in the car's handling without any electronic aids.

It is, as we have said, primarily in seemingly hopeless situations that Porsche Stability Management justifies its existence, though when in use it monitors the car's dynamic behavior permanently and with extreme accuracy. A long list of technical equipment is needed for the task:

The ABS sensors supply data on the rotating speeds of all the wheels; the alarm is only given if differences in their speeds are suddenly detected.

The steering column sensors detect the steering angle – not only to sense when the car is being cornered, but also in conjunction with other measured data such as the wheel speed differential and the

Whereas the car remains stable on a wet surface with PSM in use (large photo, left) it 'loses its grip' without this electronic co-pilot (photos above) when the curve radius becomes too tight or too much power is applied. The Porsche Turbo, although a stable car, then describes various pirouettes before even the skilled driver can ease back the gas pedal and take corrective action

Porsche Stability Management (PSM): sensors and other components

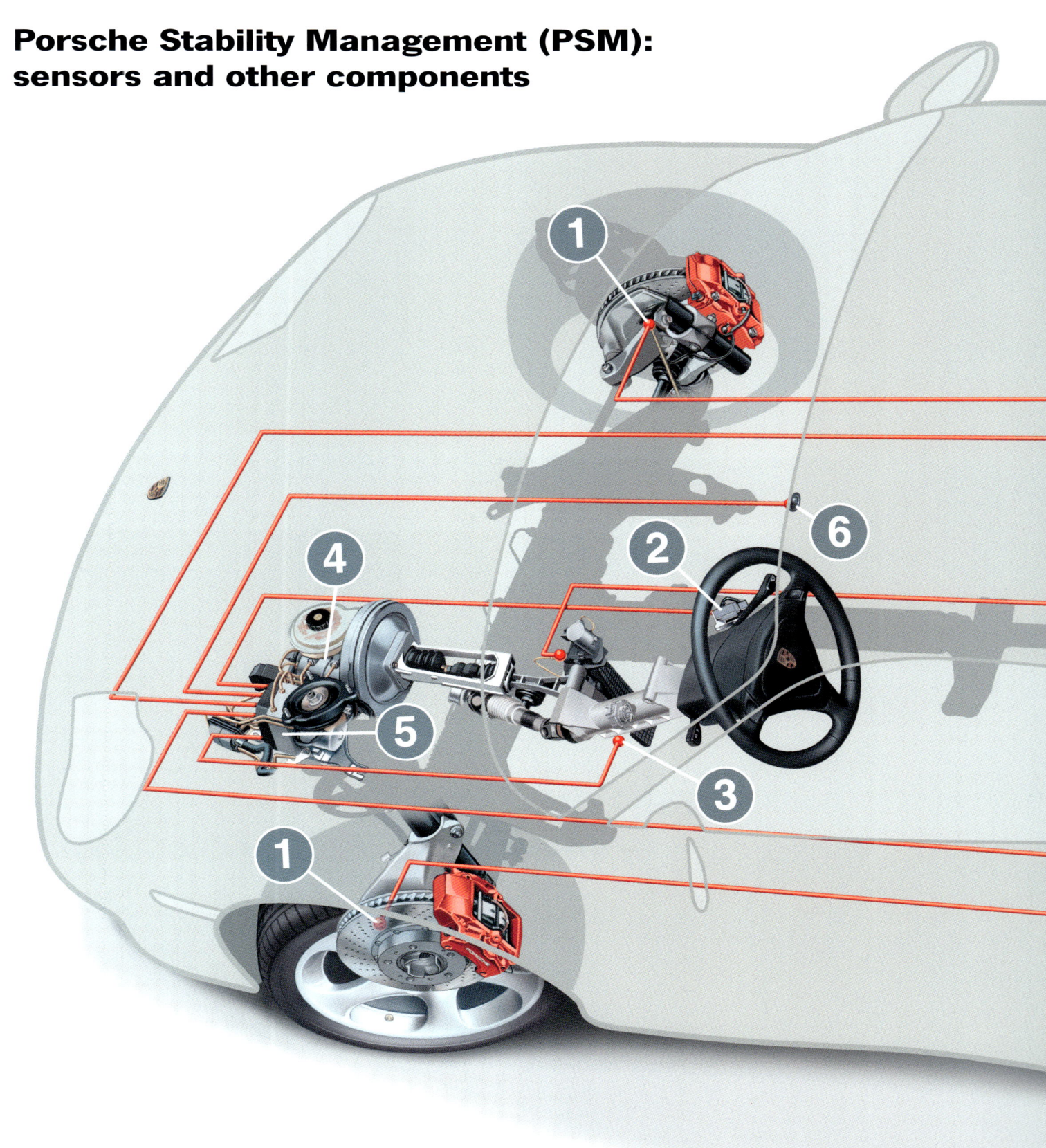

1. Wheel speed sensor
2. Integral yaw speed and lateral acceleration sensor
3. Steering angle sensor
4. Brake hydraulics preload pump

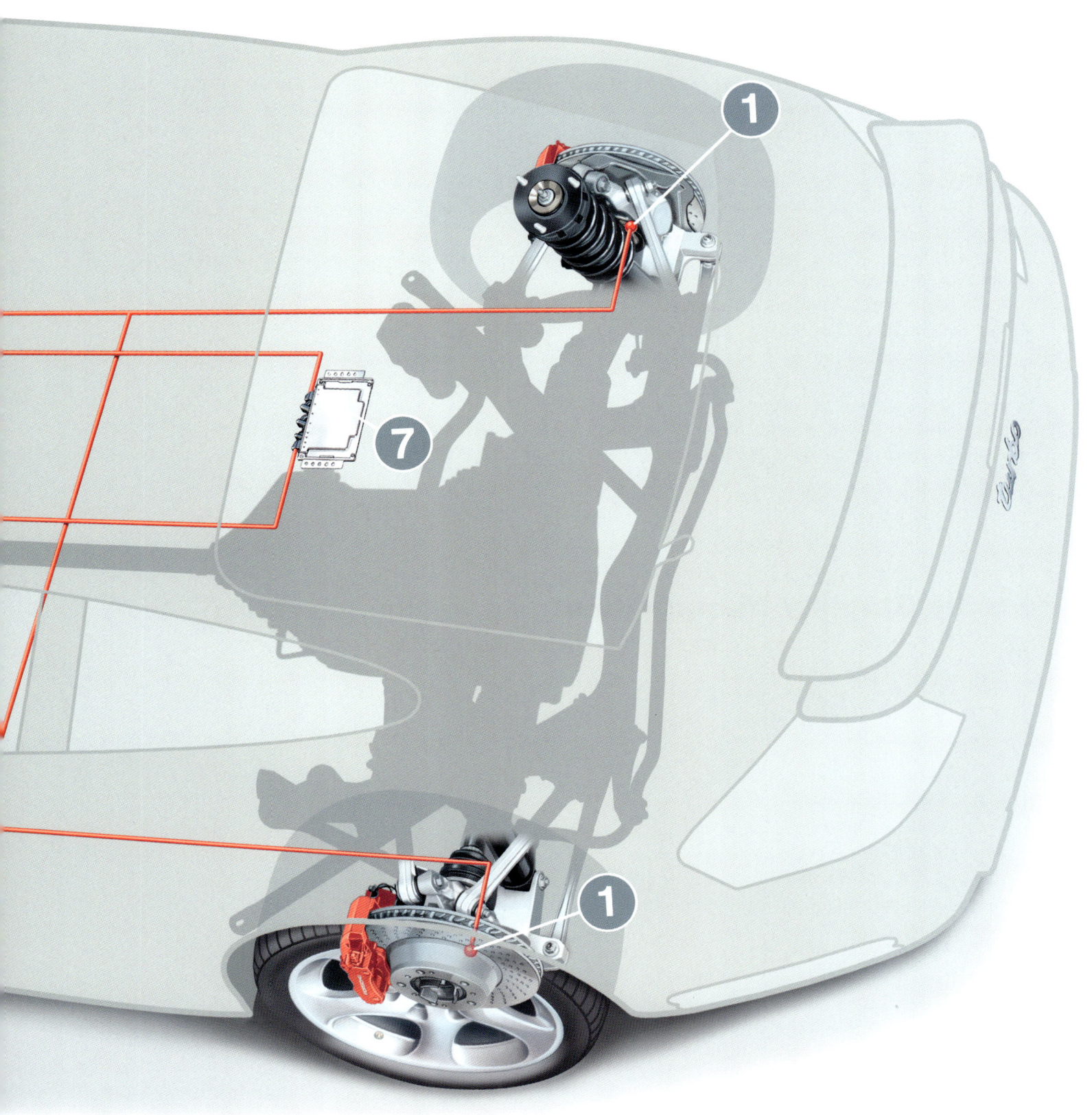

5   PSM 5.7 hydraulic pump assembly
     with pressure sensor and control unit
6   PSM switch
7   Motronic engine-management control unit

lateral acceleration value to determine whether the curve radius corresponds with the chosen steering angle. Any deviations indicate that severe under-or oversteer has set in. A further sensor for lateral acceleration is used to sense when the car begins to approach the adhesion limit. Last but not least, PSM has a 'yaw angle accelerometer' that detects an increased rate of rotary movement around the car's vertical axis – another sign of incipient oversteer or the start of a spin.

The sensor signals are transmitted to a computer which evaluates them and, if any critical values are found, takes remedial action within a few thousandths of a second. How can PSM put things right? There are two possible approaches:

It can reduce engine output by means of the 'drive-by-wire' gas pedal, regardless of how determinedly the driver keeps his or her foot down.

It can begin to apply any one of the four wheel brakes separately in order to correct the car's handling, or both rear brakes in order to restore traction at the rear wheels.

What effect does all this have in practise? If the car becomes unstable on a low-grip surface, PSM closes the throttle. If this is not enough and the car departs from the chosen line, it tries to correct this by applying the brakes as necessary.

If the car runs wide on a bend, in other words suffers from severe understeer, PSM brakes the inner rear wheel so that the car again corners more sharply.

Porsche Stability Management gets the Turbo back into line faster than any driver could lift off the gas pedal

If on the contrary the tail swings wide, then this is a bad case of oversteer, whereupon PSM applies the brake at the outer front wheel.

And this is the whole secret: PSM can apply each of the car's four road-wheel brakes separately, something that no driver could be expected to do even if such a facility were provided. Even before the driver's skill and experience get to grips with a tricky situation, PSM takes over and keeps the Porsche pointing approximately where it was intended to go.

Add Professor Processor to the team that looks after your car, and you can relax a little. The best proof of the computer's capabilities comes, oddly enough, from Formula 1 and several other categories of motor racing, where the rules forbid all such forms of electronic assistance. Why? Simply because the public would presumably prefer to see the driver win the race, not the computer.

13

Turbo boost and some of the ways of explaining it to potential customers

DOES THE TURBO NEED A MESSAGE?

By Michael Köckritz

THE TEASER

A magnificent baroque church organ with drums and trumpets. Start the new Porsche 911 Turbo, it seems to say, and the music starts too. Special occasions need to be illustrated in special ways. What more supreme way of communicating supreme sound, and the power that lies behind it. This was a teaser campaign that everyone understood, as the immediate rise in advance orders confirmed – but not only that ...

Chapter 13

IN THE BEGINNING IS NOT A WORD on most occasions, but a whole question. This is at least true of communication. Everything there begins with the question: "What do I want to say about my product?"

After the usual lengthy brainstorming sessions the specialists in this area may have black rings under their eyes, but with average luck they may also have come up with a 'core message' that gets across in a credible manner and can be used as the central communication topic to support the product's marketing objective. How easy it all was!

It becomes easier still if the product happens to have strongly marked features that no other competitor's product can match – or what the language communication calls a 'unique selling proposition' or 'USP'.

In the Porsche company's communication language, there's a more straightforward term for this: 'Turbo'. The resulting core message is then easy to formulate: Porsche's top model and therefore the best sports car there is.

Porsche introduced its first 911 Turbo in 1974 and demonstrated most impressively how a product could be positioned on the market without ingenious advertising strategies provided that it created a certain aura when arriving and departing, possessed the necessary technical substance – and could find its way directly into the hearts of the people. Since that very first combination of turbocharged 260-horsepower engine and rear-wheel drive, people have known fairly accurately what the term 'Turbo' stands for.

And today? Today the Porsche 911 Turbo has become the one model in the entire automobile world

"The magic formula for the Turbo is what we call 'integrated communication'. We have grouped all our communication measures together and co-ordinated them most carefully. This enables the core Turbo message to penetrate every area. Wherever you meet the Turbo in our communication, you immediately say to yourself: 'Here it is, the world's finest sports car!'"

Felix Bräutigam, Porsche's Marketing Communication Manager

that doesn't even need to be illustrated to get the message across. We have now reached the level of 'general Turbo communication': the first ad in the latest 911 Turbo campaign, for instance, has a picture of a splendid baroque church organ with, underneath it, the briefest of all copy: "*The new 911 Turbo is coming.* Period. Nothing else – but everyone who sees it say "Wow!" and wakes up immediately. Felix Bräutigam, Head of Porsche's Marketing Communication and therefore responsible for corporate advertising, says so, and he should know. Agreed, the sheer extent of the reactions to this ad has surprised even the most experienced communication expert.

"We knew immediately that this was a blockbuster of an ad, one that was bound to have the effect we wanted," says Anton Hunger, Head of Porsche's Press and Public Affairs. It was anticipated that impatient journalists and potential Turbo customers would reach for the telephone and ask when the 'new one' was scheduled to appear.

What nobody expected were so many calls from a variety of other people: organ-builders, for example. Organ recital organizers, organ photographers, organ music publishers – and of course organists too! Anton Hunger smiles a little shamefacedly: "Six months ago, I would have never believed that Porsche would be sponsoring organ music or that our company magazine Christophorus would publish a

Chapter 13

PRESENTATION ...

*Those who do a good deed are not only entitled to talk about it,
as the saying goes, but are allowed to invite critical experts
to drive it too! That's what press driving events are for*

long article on organs!' He believes it now – and is very happy with the situation, since it is always his aim to strengthen Porsche's social acceptance among broad sections of the public. Hunger: "No-one who buys a Porsche should have to justify the decision. For this reason our communication work never concentrates solely on appealing to potential customers by way of the product itself. We try to convey the full extent of the claim we make, the achievements of our engineers and the philosophy that lies behind it – and therefore the feeling for life that is inseparably linked with our sports cars."

Porsche's communication experts are on the right track. The latest image studies also confirm this. They show most impressively that not only is the media trend as far as Porsche's brand and product presentation is concerned very positive, not to say euphoric, but that the brand profile as a whole is convincing. It also fits into the overall picture admirably when, for instance, Porsche is chosen by Germany's managers as the company with the highest current reputation. That Porsche is among

Anton Hunger (right), head of Porsche's Press and Public Affairs department, welcomes journalists to the international Porsche 911 Turbo press driving event in Carmona, held as usual shortly before the new model's market launch. Porsche doesn't accompany such occasions with a great deal of unnecessary pomp and circumstance. The cars are allowed to speak for themselves. The entire Turbo presentation takes place in a restrained, professional atmosphere with the product as the center of interest

The Porsche company's image in the media has been stable at a very positive level for some time now; this was recently reflected in the choice of Porsche as the company in Germany with the highest reputation ('manager magazin')

... AND OPINION

the favorite automobile brands is something that we have suspected for some time even without an opinion poll.

These surveys and assessments were conducted before the latest Turbo arrived on the scene. Porsche's image took off yet again when the extra thrust of Turbo communication had its proper effect. To achieve the best possible result, Porsche's PR and advertising professionals grouped their resources and tools together at an early stage and coordinated them closely. The Porsche motor sport department would probably call this 'fine tuning', but for all concerned the magic formula is 'integrated

ADVERTISING MOTIFS ...

Compromises are there to satisfy everyone. This time, we decided to think only of you.

The new 911 Turbo.

communication'. It takes a suitably concentrated, all-embracing approach to make optimum use of all synergies and multiplier effects and to render the core message of the best of all sports cars transparent, convincing and credible. In any case, the new Porsche 911 Turbo transmits values such as sporting character, innovative technology, design, authenticity and individuality with particular strength, in other words all the familiar Porsche corporate and brand signals – which makes it the ideal image-carrier, with a technical claim pattern and the associated lines of experience surpassing any other 'hallo effect' that the Porsche brand could conceivably wish for.

Felix Bräutigam, head of Porsche's Marketing Communication department, explains: "This is why the communication concept for the Turbo has nothing to do with the volume of cars we plan to sell. Our strategy is aimed at utilizing the enthusiasm that the new 911 Turbo stimulates to maintain the high level of interest and enthusiasm that the Porsche brand enjoys."

   A spinoff effect is that a broader target group is created for the entire product program. Bräutigam: "This makes Porsche a realistic 'dream brand' for a larger group of customers."

   A supreme sports car is naturally one thing, its supreme presentation as a product is quite another.

   It's important to know that human beings have a strong tendency to allow themselves to be deflected from what they are supposed to be concentrating on – just one of those disastrous human flaws we none the less seem to be able to live with. Take advertising, for example. Instead of making a careful mental note of the sports car in the ad and checking where the nearest dealer is to be found, contact with even the most carefully conceived advertising is so often broken off prematurely – for what reason?

Chapter 13

... AND THE PRESS

Pictures are one of the quickest and most effective methods of communication. The human brain processes them more rapidly and thoroughly, and they also have an initial eye-catching effect. Porsche's 911 Turbo communication therefore concentrates strictly on the pictorial image, with the car itself playing the leading role. The background is used only to give the car its logical presence

Usually to turn the page, zap to the next channel or listen to what someone else is saying – depending on the chosen advertising medium.

Advertising can't survive an elaborate communicative lead-up. Today, it's the 'quickie' that hits the target. Companies have no more than three to four seconds on average to convey their message in a double-page advertisement, two seconds for a single page and even less when they only have half a page at their disposal. Just imagine: the consumer has the audacity to discard our carefully thought-out ad after a single second has elapsed! Even the finest sports cars aren't immune to this law of the jungle.

But we want the reader to get at least some impression of the product, the brand and our achievements, don't we? In view of this, wouldn't it be better to pack the supposed target group one by one into a Porsche 911 Turbo and give them a direct sample of what they are missing? In the time they spend looking at a two-page advertisement we could whisk them up from a standstill to almost a hundred kilometers an hour and they would also acquire a very clear and definite picture of the Porsche idea and the top Porsche's performance.

Chapter 13

There's another very frequently encountered risk too: the reader or viewer is so fascinated by the blonde model in her miniskirt, who those clever advertising strategists just happen to have posed next to the actual product, that our 'time is up' before we have looked our fill. So much for eye-catchers in sparsely cut outfits.

Porsche knows the mechanisms of human nature as well as anybody; for years, classic Porsche Turbo advertising has dispensed with all forms of 'sexaggerated' effect, and concentrated on essentials. The car itself and the lasting experience it generates – these are the core messages. The visual images are reduced in complexity and focussed strongly on the car, until every detail becomes clear. The design of the 911 Turbo is entirely capable of speaking for itself. Every aspect of it has a function, and the form follows it in the classic way as the visible consequence of what the car can actually do. What more logical conclusion, therefore, than to make it the main element in visual communication.

"We use the background only as an additional means of introducing an emotive element," says Felix Bräutigam. The car, in this case the Turbo, is our sole hero. The copy is kept short and direct: its tone emphasizes the reference status enjoyed by the Porsche Turbo and displays the Porsche badge in close proximity to the Porsche name. Credibility presented with a degree of understatement: the act of communication itself must be in accord with Porsche's corporate philosophy. And Porsche, after all, is led by passionate engineers.

Just another brief reference to credibility. When the readers of the leading German car magazine 'auto motor und sport' chose their car of the year for 2000, they voted the new Porsche 911 Turbo into first place as 'best sports car' although this model had not even been presented to the public at the time. They chose the Porsche Carrera as its runner-up. This tells us two things: that the Turbo is regarded by the public as Porsche's top model, and that this evidently makes it the best sports car in the world.

Sometimes the core message takes on a life of its own. Particularly if the USP happens to bear the name 'Turbo'.

A technical masterpiece ought to make its effect where it belongs. On the road

Chapter 14

A DAY WITH A THOUSAND CURVES

By Michael Köckritz

The only proper way to appreciate a great sports car is to drive it yourself – or let Walter Röhrl do the driving for you!

Chapter 14

THE DIGITAL INTERIOR TEMPERATURE DISPLAY READS 20 degrees Centigrade, a pleasant enough figure, but it's ceased to have any meaning for me. My body temperature seems to have gone out of control at about the same time as the synthetic oil in the engine's dry sump reached its correct operating temperature. When did I begin to feel this way? By the third corner on our first lap! Since then I have been hot, there's no other words for it. Yet I'm not doing anything, am I?

I'm just the passenger, and my only task is to grip the edge of the seat, the door pull or any other convenient object inside the car with quiet desperation at increasingly frequent intervals. I tend to do this when we're taking a corner. Here comes one now ... we're hurtling at well over 125 miles an hour into a series of tight bends that I would never have dreamed of tackling at even a fraction of this speed. Left to myself, I would have stamped on the brake pedal a long time ago. Curiously enough, my driver shows no signs of doing so. I decide to help him out, with both feet, while he finishes explaining in a supremely relaxed way that the "character of the new Porsche 911 Turbo is largely defined by the driving experience". About five seconds later Röhrl has braked, rather late in my humble opinion but very determinedly indeed. A sigh of relief escapes me as I become aware of what he means. After a further fifteen minutes have elapsed, I am absolutely sure.

It takes time to get accustomed to 420 horsepower of the most vigorous kind and the amazingly efficient way they can be transmitted to the road. It's a rare privilege to be allowed to see Walter Röhrl probing the

132
133

Controllability came late to the Turbo, but it has no weaknesses in that area now

134 *Everything in or on the Turbo has a practical function to perform*
135

First and foremost it is the unbelievable thrust from the turbocharged engine that sticks in the memory. Later one discovers that this is a splendid car in which to cover long distances in a truly satisfying manner

identity of this precision power package, establishing a passionate relationship with it and exploring all the delights it offers the skilled driver. With eyes wide open, one sits metaphorically at least at his feet and recalls scraps of what one learned in school about moving bodies and their dynamic limits. Later, on the road, one treats the Porsche Turbo with the respect it has earned.

Röhrl, twice world rally champion, directs the new four-wheel-drive sports car around our test track with the lightest of hands. Accelerating through a gentle S-bend in fourth gear as if on rails, he remarks: "There was a time when it was difficult to steer a straight course in the Turbo, but today it's just as easy as in a car with the engine at the front." Evidently it is. With the typical throaty voice of Porsche's water-cooled six behind us, we hurtle towards the horizon as if pulled by an invisible strand of rubber – straight as an arrow, even though the road surface is wavy and uneven at this point. If a fight is taking place, I can't see it: Röhrl holds the steering wheel calmly in his hands and the car pursues the line he has chosen without the slightest objection.

The same corners were distinctly more exciting in earlier Turbo seasons. The 260-horsepower model from the nineteen-seventies was about as amenable as an angry bucking bronco compared with this.

Chapter 14

Röhrl remembers: "You took it into the corner, put your foot hard down and waited to see if you had everything under control or not – the power used to come in so brutally!" We know that even then Röhrl had everything under control, in contrast to many of the less experienced sports-car owners who would fling their Turbo into the next corner with a carefree gesture, only to find that the road surface under the wheels had mysteriously changed into grass. Such enforced excursions should have given them ample opportunity for wondering what exactly they had done wrong, but many of them have probably still not found the answer. Those were the days when the Porsche Turbo commanded a different kind of respect.

Today's Turbo conjures up such on-the-limit situations largely in the minds of apprehensive passengers. Porsche's attitude to performance is to hone and polish it to perfection, and the new 911 Turbo is a further notable landmark along this path. Agreed, one is still confronted suddenly with limits, but they are one's own, not the car's, and this is how things should be. Although my shirt is well and truly damp around the collar, I am beginning to enjoy being a part of the Röhrl-plus-Turbo machine. The former rally champion not only opens up entirely new concepts of mobility for my struggling brain but is also a brilliantly informative guide to the technical features and engineering achievements that lie behind them.

Like its immediate predecessor, the new 911 Turbo has four-wheel drive. Depending on the driving situation this diverts up to 40 percent of the twin-turbo engine's enormous power to the front wheels, through a multi-disk viscous coupling that smooths out the power and torque peaks. Porsche's objective was not

New headlamps and a bold front air dam with wider fenders give the 911 Turbo its own visual character. Bi-xenon headlights illuminate the road effectively after dark

140 / **141** *This is what half a mobile family tree looks like! The first 260-hp generation leads the way here, followed by Turbo models from 1995 and 2000*

merely optimum traction: the Turbo's four-wheel drive is basically a technical device adopted to give the car its outstanding road behaviour in all circumstances and an exceptionally high safety level whenever the handling limits are approached.

The new 911 Turbo was certainly not conceived with the tunnel vision of the top-speed maniac. 4.2 seconds from 0 to 100 km/h (62 mph), 9.2 equally entertaining seconds to 160 km/h (100 mph) and a top speed of 305 kilometers an hour (almost 190 miles an hour) are somehow no more than the logical consequences of an efficient design approach. For those who produced the Porsche 911 Turbo, the requirement was to ensure that such tremendous performance potential is always under perfect control. No mean task with a torque of 560 Newton-meters waiting at the rear to be transmitted safely to the road at an engine speed of only 2,700 rpm, or when the waste gates of the turbochargers reach their pressure limit of 1.80 bar and the car's occupants are well aware that something special is happening.

Porsche has responded to the need not to tame the Turbo's sheer performance but at least to keep it in check in unfavorable circumstances. The initials PSM stand for Porsche Stability Management, an electronic guardian angel who seems to know what the driver had in mind even when the car itself doesn't. Precision sensors measure road-wheel speeds, steering angle, lateral forces and acceleration around the vertical axis, identify left or right corners and determine the extent to which the car is responding to the driver's wishes.

Chapter 14

If the Turbo should slide or skid in extreme circumstances, PSM (which can be switched off if not needed) applies a single wheel brake to stabilize it again. If the car oversteers and the tail threatens to swing wide, the outer front wheel is braked and counteracts the car's tendency to spin. If this isn't enough, PSM also reduces engine power regardless of the electronic accelerator pedal's actual opening angle.

This is Röhrl's cue to demonstrate how effectively a combination of four-wheel drive, PSM, sport spring and shock absorber settings and a body lowered by ten millimeters (four tenths of an inch) can be when any such difficult driving situation arises. The electronics apply the brakes very smoothly and provide the driver with a certain amount of scope for personal action even when the laws of physics are stretched to their limit. Walter Röhrl, one of those drivers who have learned to steer the car with the gas pedal, naturally welcomes this decision on Porsche's part.

He also comments that although he isn't a great one for braking and is only likely to activate the anti-lock braking system about five times a year at the very most, he nevertheless finds the latest Turbo's brakes extremely impressive. Their construction principle isn't new: it was thoroughly proved in the Porsche Carrera, but in view of the Turbo's leading-edge performance the four-piston aluminum calipers at the front and rear wheels are distinctly larger and even more powerful.

The ventilated, cross-drilled brake disks are now 330 millimeters (13 inches) in diameter and rated for exceptional performance in the toughest imaginable conditions. Despite this, Porsche has resolved to make them even better from the late fall of 2000 on, by offering its customers composite ceramic brake disks with

The limits which suddenly confront you are not the car's but your own

a revolutionary internal cooling system. These can be retrofitted to existing cars and are appearing for the first time in any automobile manufacturer's catalog. They will raise sports-car braking standards higher still in terms of initial response, resistance to fading, operating life and low weight. Such an epoch-making development naturally deserves a name of its own, and Porsche has therefore decided on 'Porsche Ceramic Composite Brake' (PCCB) for this new, highly effective system.

Another feature that no earlier 911 Turbo was able to offer is the five-speed Tiptronic S transmission. It is an alternative now to the standard six-speed stick-shift gearbox, and an entirely new development. Any potential Turbo customers who fear that the car's dynamism will be sacrificed can rest assured: Porsche's transmission specialists have fed all the necessary shift strategies into the electronic control unit in such a way that the shift points are varied instantly to suit the driving style and the road conditions sensed by the system.

Walter Röhrl is a man of few words. Say what you have to say, is his motto. This makes his verdict all the more credible: "The Turbo is the best sports car there is!" I believe him.

My shirt is almost dry again. I relax in the passenger seat and even consider turning the temperature control up slightly. I don't expect Walter Röhrl to raise any objections!

Berlin's bear is a symbol of strength – like the Porsche Turbo

15

TWO EVERGREENS, EACH IN ITS OWN TYPICAL WAY. The Porsche Turbo, the subject of this book, is now in its fifth generation and first saw the light of day in 1974. Berlin has been around since 1244, if we are to believe the documents their historians produce. The car and the city have something else in common: a series of ups and downs in their history.

Take the last of the 'old' Turbo models, for instance. It had a 3.6-liter, 408-horsepower air-cooled engine and went out of production in April 1998. The clock that recorded its fascinating combination of power, boost pressure and passion stopped abruptly after counting 32,223 cars off the assembly line since Porsche introduced its first forced-aspiration 911, the 'Ur-Turbo' so to speak. The message to the lovers of this car held out a modicum of hope: keep calm, the next one will be along in two years' time.

In Berlin, people had to wait a whole lot longer and their situation was so much more serious as to make such comparisons seem trivial. The city on the green banks of the Spree in which millions live spent forty years, no less, in a state of urban trance – politically, economically and also in terms of its appearance. In all those years of enforced division, Berlin never managed to build up any boost pressure of its own; the task of resisting the pressures exerted on it from the outside was hard enough.

The wall that split Berlin into two parts was as unsightly as a deliberate scratch on the paint on a fine car; it disfigured the one flawless image of an eternal city deliberately and, so its perpetrators felt, permanently. This ugly scar has been reemoved, it is a thing of the past, though not forgotten.

STOUT HEARTS AND NEW HORIZONS

By Malte Jürgens

Dynamic, with a powerful heartbeat, a legend in its time, it is flexing its muscles in 2000 for a journey into the future

New, pulsating life now courses through the veins of Germany's old and new capital city. The country and the people have taken new heart from the change that has come upon them. Sometimes they break the rules a little, boom-town style, just to see what happens. This we can surely forgive them, since the urge forward is so splendidly dynamic – as indeed it is with the Porsche Turbo. Politics and business reap the benefit, but so do altogether more elegant areas of art and culture, urban encounter and the avant-garde lifestyle.

There is one constant factor in the world of Berlin: variety. Nowhere is this more evident than in its architectural ideals, which extend from the historic tradition of such master-builders as Friedrich Schinkel to the ultra-modern structures of Zaha Hadid. The background commentary to such developments has always been delivered free of charge by the natives of Berlin, renowned as they are for a turbocharged mixture of satire and inventiveness.

So many of the city's imposing structures have been kept squarely on the ground by the nicknames bestowed on them. The nave and tower of the new Emperor Wilhelm Memorial Church: for the locals, they are 'Lipstick and Powder Compact'. The advanced ferro-concrete structure of the earlier Congress Hall? The 'pregnant Oyster'! New material for the Berliners' sharp but not unkind tongue is springing up all over: the 'Reichstag' government building with its new glass dome, the concrete tower blocks that have erupted from

Chapter 15

the ground at Potsdamer Platz – no doubt some superlative new labels are being attached to them at this very moment. We shall see – and is that other superlative, the Porsche Turbo, likely to escape?

A remake of a great city and the latest remake of a legendary automobile – under a glass-fiber parabola the Porsche legend awaits its admirers. Where better than Berlin to look for a stimulating backdrop for such a pedigree, full-throttle car? The mystique of the Turbo is derived from ultimately logical, not to say common-sense features: excellent performance, supreme reliability, brakes that grip quite monstrously well, maintenance intervals that have been extended year by year. Turbocharged power wrapped in a cocoon of magnificent, high-quality craftsmanship and crowned with an evergreen winner's laurels from the Le Mans 24-hour race, for instance the 1998 overall victory by the Porsche GT1.

A weightless spin-off, the Porsche legend accompanies us on our trip through boom-town Berlin like an invisible passenger, a high-octane cloud of fame and honor that floats above this 420-horsepower coupé on the first much-admired stages of our journey. What's stopping the right foot from giving the gas pedal a real hard push? Nothing, unless it be the need to warm over eleven quarts of synthetic engine oil in the dry sump lube system first.

Hemmed in by serried ranks of 30-mile limit signs, the thrill of commanding so much power dwindles to the still satisfactory feeling that 'if one wanted to, one could!' The Turbo condescends to stay within the

146 *Pull down the wall and may the power be with you: times are changing at 'turbo tempo' in Berlin*

144 *Two symbols of freedom: once again the Brandenburg Gate links East and West, and invites*
145 *the Turbo to start its latest journey*

law and rolls restrainedly from the Grosser Stern to the Brandenburg Gate, smooth and cultured in its manner, with no shake, no jerking or misfiring – a high-tech mobile created by a gifted sculptor, with the Tiergarten as its setting. A low-slung red counterpoint to the massive granite artworks in the Sculpture Park between the old Congress Hall and the new Chancellery. A mirror, symbol or metaphor for the progress of a city and of the cars that dwell in it.
The two KKK turbochargers deliver the famous Berlin air to the combustion chambers with only mild boost pressure, at least for the moment. We want the rest of this celebrated air to stay as clean as possible, and so the Turbo's exhaust system has very large, highly-efficient catalytic converters with metal monoliths and complies with the tough limits laid down by the D4 exhaust emission regulations – which makes it one of the cleanest characters around in some parts of Germany's capital city.

A short pause in front of one of Berlin's principal landmarks: the Brandenburg Gate, built in 1791 by Carl Gotthard Langhans in the style of an Ancient Greek propyleum, is 85 feet high and 213 feet wide. It's a symbol of determination, of persistence, robbed of the quadriga surmounting it by Napoleon the First as early as 1807. Later it was damaged in war, shut away, restored and re-opened – an authentic reminder of the times we have lived in.

What a contrast to the latest manifestation of targeted forward mobility, hardly more than 50 inches high and 72 inches wide. The length too, is a compact 175 inches, negligible in comparison with the 50 feet of

152 / **153** *Sources of power: the Federal German Parliament meets in the old Reichstag building, and 420 hp await us outside*

the Brandenburg Gate's Doric stone columns. But there is consistent design here too: the Turbo's silhouette still echoes the golden mean of the very first sketches a quarter of a century ago – a noteworthy achievement at a time when every manufacturer's styling department throughout the world is striving frenetically to carve out a new niche for itself in automobile history.

Agreed, the fenders follow a slightly smoother line now, the bi-xenon headlamps curve gracefully down into the bumper and the characteristic rear wing is no longer quite the shallow tea-tray below the rear window that once struck awe into us. Now it has a high-tech telescopic action and extends automatically when the car reaches 75 miles per hour. But this 2+2-seater coupé still communicates the same visual strength as ever: the most exotic flower of the species 911 cries out as always for our attention.

Precise power steering with a wonderfully light action, an easy-to-operate single dry plate clutch and the six-speed gearbox with a specially reinforced wire cable shift mechanism – they make the new Turbo perfectly capable of tolerating an aimless drive through city streets. The six-cylinder engine with its twin turbochargers, an elaborate boost pressure control system and VarioCam Plus valve timing control runs silkily at even the low speeds called for in town.

Press the electronic 'power-by-wire' gas pedal down, however, and the rear engine leaps into life determinedly and without the slightest hint of temperament. There's no lag, but neither does the power come in violently enough to take the driver aback . With the cool confidence that comes from having a maximum of

158

159

Wide-throttle stroller and perfect gentleman: even when beset by urban speed limits the new Turbo remains a civilized companion

154
155
Old memories: when the war had swept over the walls of Berlin, Porsche's sports-car history took off with the VW Beetle as its starting point

560 Newton-meters of torque available without having to exceed 2,700 revolutions per minute, the red road runner thrusts its way along the boulevards of Berlin, happy to be giving its driver such rare pleasure.

Those who are bored with all that gear-shift and clutch work at the red lights and in the capital city's stop-and-go traffic can order the new Turbo with a revised version of Porsche's Tiptronic S five-speed automatic transmission. Its electronic shift programs have a number of ingenious ideas in reserve, from a specific warm-up routine to heat up the catalysts without delay, through suppression of upshifts if the throttles are closed suddenly, and retention of the chosen gear when cornering.

The car's four-wheel drive, already tried with success in the Carrera 4, is also an intelligent system: by way of a viscous coupling at the input to the front-axle final drive, it diverts at least five and at most forty percent of the engine's power to the steered wheels if the need arises. Even a quick visit to one of Berlin's many construction sites around the new parliament building are not likely to lead to the embarrassment of spinning to a halt in the sand – on which we must hope that our politicians have not built the new city center.

In Berlin's new amusement area between Oranienburger Strasse and the Hackesche Höfe, accurate navigation is needed between the rows of less than neatly parked vehicles outside the innumerable bars, but unlike many another prize nocturnal specimen, our Turbo never loses its head.

The hoarse whisper of the six-cylinder is the ideal entry ticket for such bizarre watering-holes, where lesser guests could find their way barred by smartly dressed ladies who imply that a private party is in progress. Passers-by turn their heads, note the curved triangular exhaust tailpipes and nod approvingly as they read the simple lettering above them: Turbo.

Driver and Coupé have become thoroughly warm in these urban ravines lined with buildings in all stages of completion and a bevy of construction cranes. It's time for a quick spin along the tangled 'autobahns' in and around the city. The Turbo takes to the fast lane as to the manner born and catapults itself into the flow of traffic like a horizontal bungee jumper on an invisible rope. Faster and arrow-straight, this supersports car reels in the asphalt and concrete like so many strands of spaghetti.

The passing wind snatches the sound of the free-revving engine away from us. The engine owes much to the Type 964, with its vertically split crankcase and eight main bearings. The 420 horsepower it develops are not just a luxury but a delight.

Fast highway curves are taken by the Porsche with true Turbo confidence, with neutral handling secure in the firm grip of superb suspension, four-wheel drive and, if need be, Porsche Stability Management (PSM). Subject only to the laws of physics not being infringed, the computer brakes individual wheels as necessary, or gently closes the throttle to reduce power delivery from the engine.

The Turbo silhouette has not departed in a quarter of a century from the golden mean of the original sketches – a noteworthy achievement in an era when every styling department in the world is intent on carving out its own niche

We have reached the former Dessau racetrack, just beyond the River Elbe and scarcely an hour by Turbo from Berlin. If traffic permits, the magic 300 km/h (186 mph) barrier can be sampled, even exceeded. It's good to know that fade-free racing brakes can disperse the explosive kinetic energy unleashed by the Coupé and slow it at a rate that even exceeds gravitational force.

The Turbo turns its head back again toward Berlin. Our very first fling away from the lure of the big city has shown us how magnificently Porsche has succeeded in perfecting the legend.
Back on the Avus, in front of the Congress Center, flags are blowing in the night wind, among them Berlin's red-and-white banner with a rampant bear in its center. How well this grizzly but somehow amiable beast symbolizes the link between the city on the River Spree and the fast cars from farther south on the outskirts of Stuttgart. Berlin and the Turbo: what they have in common is strength.

Impressum/Credits

This book has been produced with the support of Dr. Ing. h.c. F. Porsche AG, for which our sincere thanks are due.

Publisher
This edition first published in 2000 by MBI Publishing Company, 729 Prospect Avenue, PO Box 1, Osceola, WI 54020-0001 USA

Editor
Rindlisbacher & Co., Handelsgesellschaft für Druckprodukte, Frunts, Zuoz
Co-editor: Abteilung Öffentlichkeitsarbeit der Dr. Ing. h.c. F. Porsche AG
© 2000 by Rindlisbacher & Co.

All rights reserved. With the exception of quoting brief passages for the purpose of review, no part of this publication may be reproduced without prior written permission from the publisher.

The information in this book is true and complete to the best of our knowledge. All recommendations are made without any guarantee on the part of the author or publisher, who also disclaim any liability incurred in connection with the use of this data or specific details.

We recognize that some words, model names and designations, for example, mentioned herein are the property of the trademark holder. We use them for identification purposes only.
This is not an official publication.

MBI Publishing Company books are also available at discounts in bulk quantity for industrial or sales-promotional use. For details, write to Special Sales Manager at Motorbooks International Wholesalers & Distributors, 729 Prospect Avenue, PO Box 1, Osceola, WI 54020-0001 USA.

Library of Congress Cataloging-in-Publication Data Available.

ISBN 0-7603-0965-5

Printed in Germany

Concept: Clauspeter Becker, Uli Praetor, Peter Vann

Graphic design: Uli Praetor

Project coordination at Porsche AG: Klaus Steckkönig

Translations: Colin Brazier

Photos: Peter Vann; also Christoph Bauer (page 126), Stephane Foulon (page 129),
AH Max Moritz (pages 47, 48, 50/51, 52), Dr. Ing. h.c. F. Porsche AG (pages 37, 115, 124, 128),
Joe Rusz/Road & Track (pages 42/43), Rainer Schlegelmilch (pages 23, 24/25, 30/31, 35),
Schweizer Automobilrevue (pages 40/41), H. D. Seufert/auto motor und sport (pages 44/45),
Dirk Weyhenmeyer (pages 96, 127)

Illustrations: Harm Lagaay (pages 4/5), Serge Bellu (pages 18/19, 20/21),
Dieter Ziegenfeuter/XING Art Productions (pages 38/39),
Dr. Ing. h.c. F. Porsche AG (pages 64/65, 77, 117, 120/121)

Blocks: Laudert/Vreden, Unternehmen für innovative Medientechnik

Printing: Offsetdruckerei Karl Grammlich, Pliezhausen

Bookbinding: G. Lachenmaier, Reutlingen